THE JUMBLIES
AND OTHER NONSENSE VERSES

WITH DRAWINGS BY
L·LESLIE BROOKE

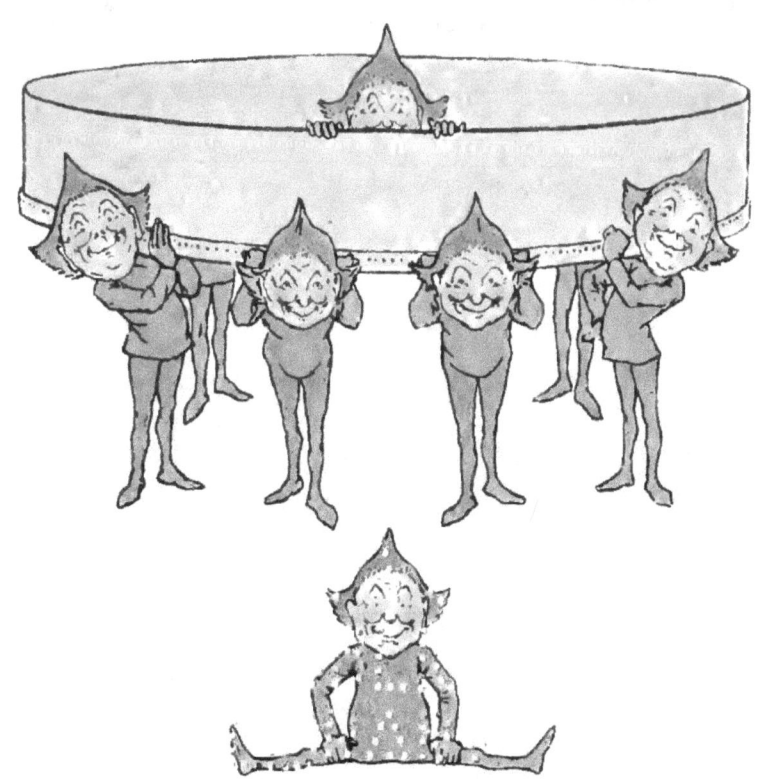

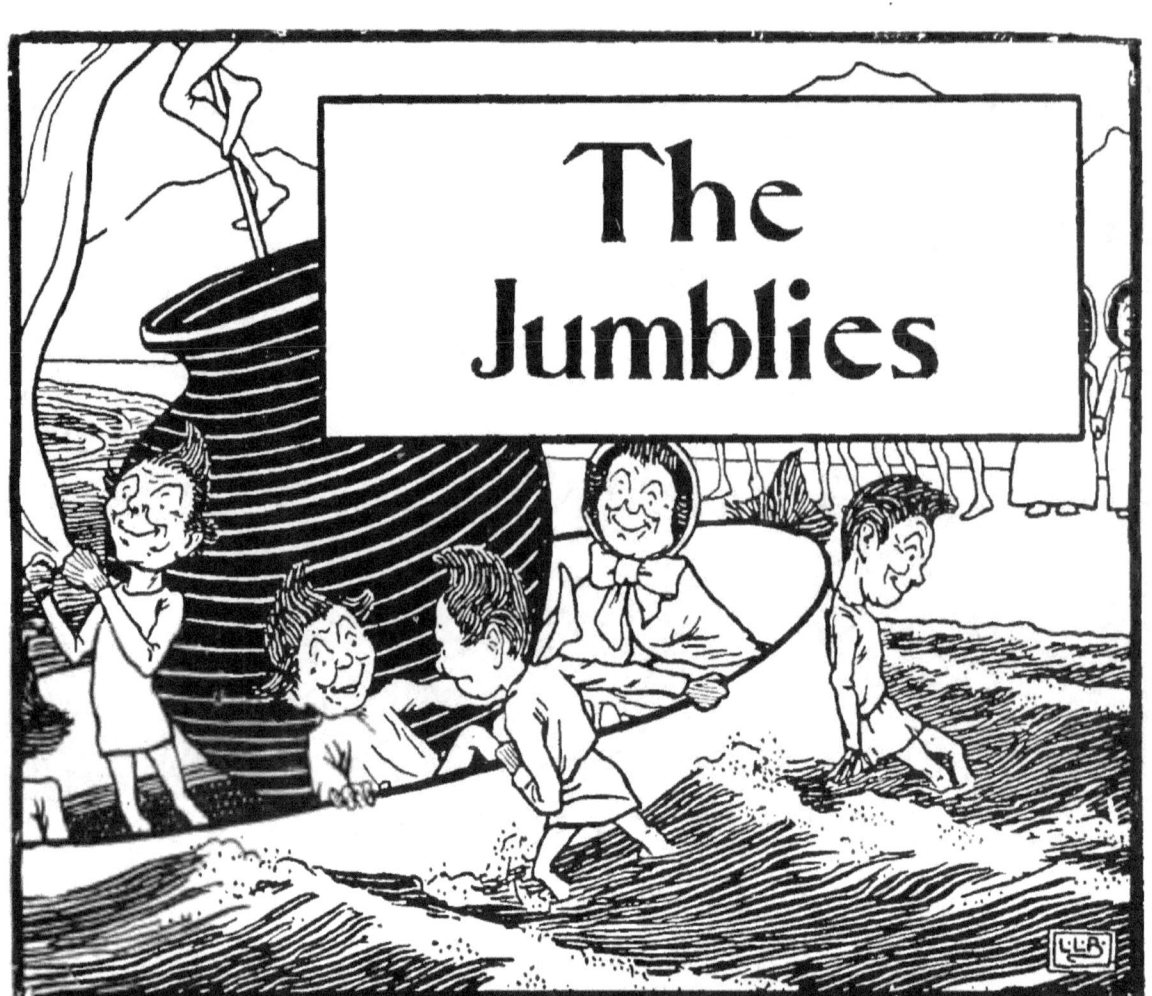

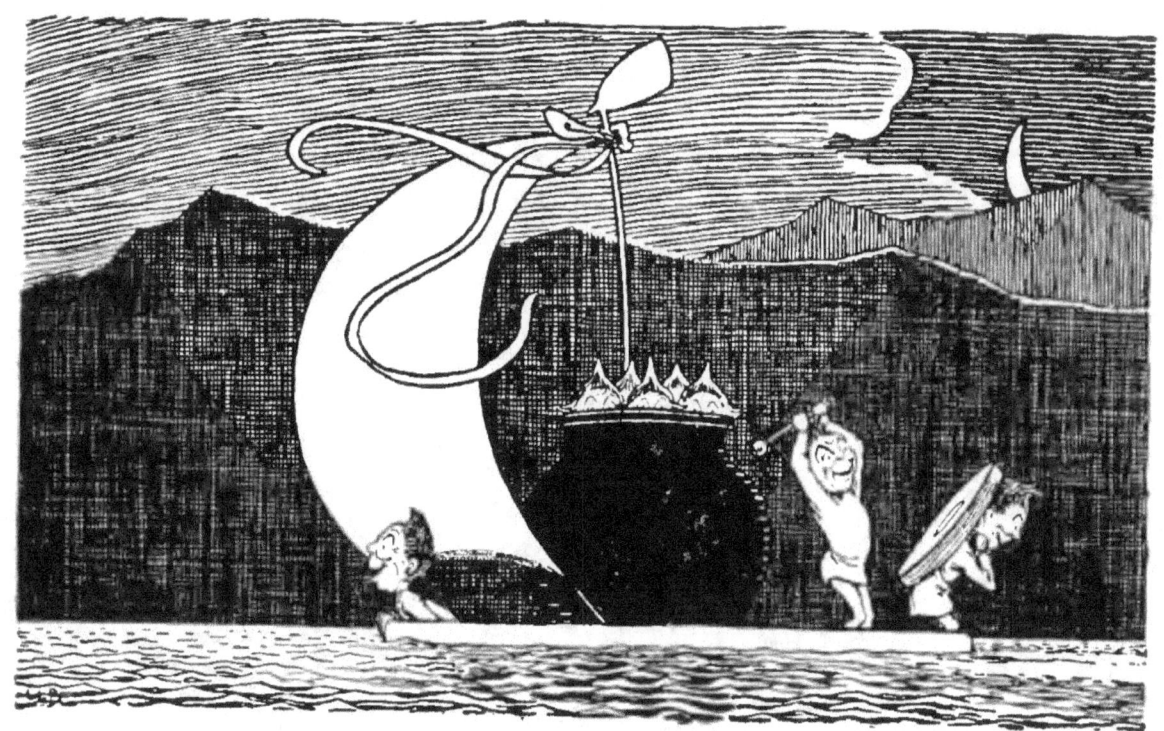

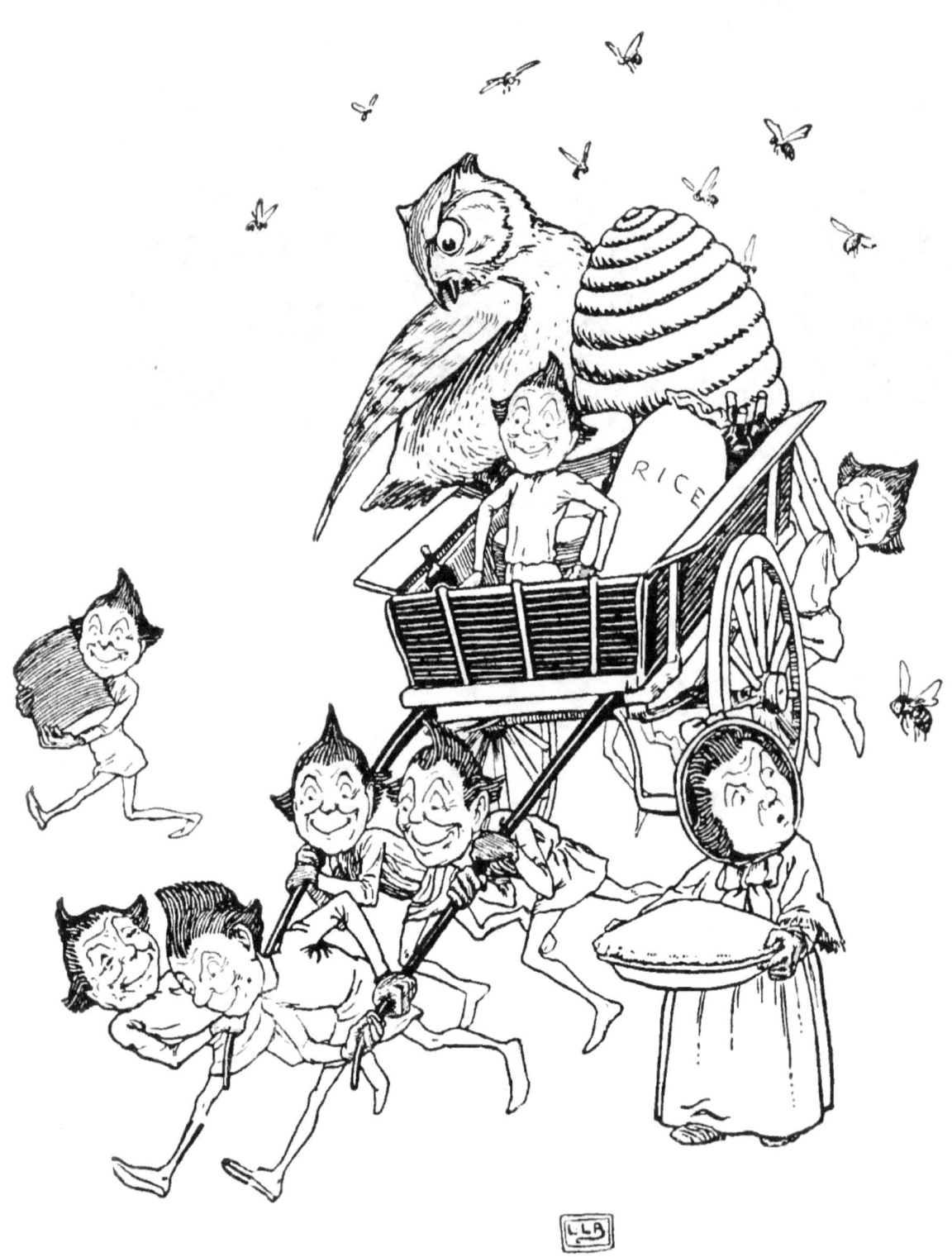

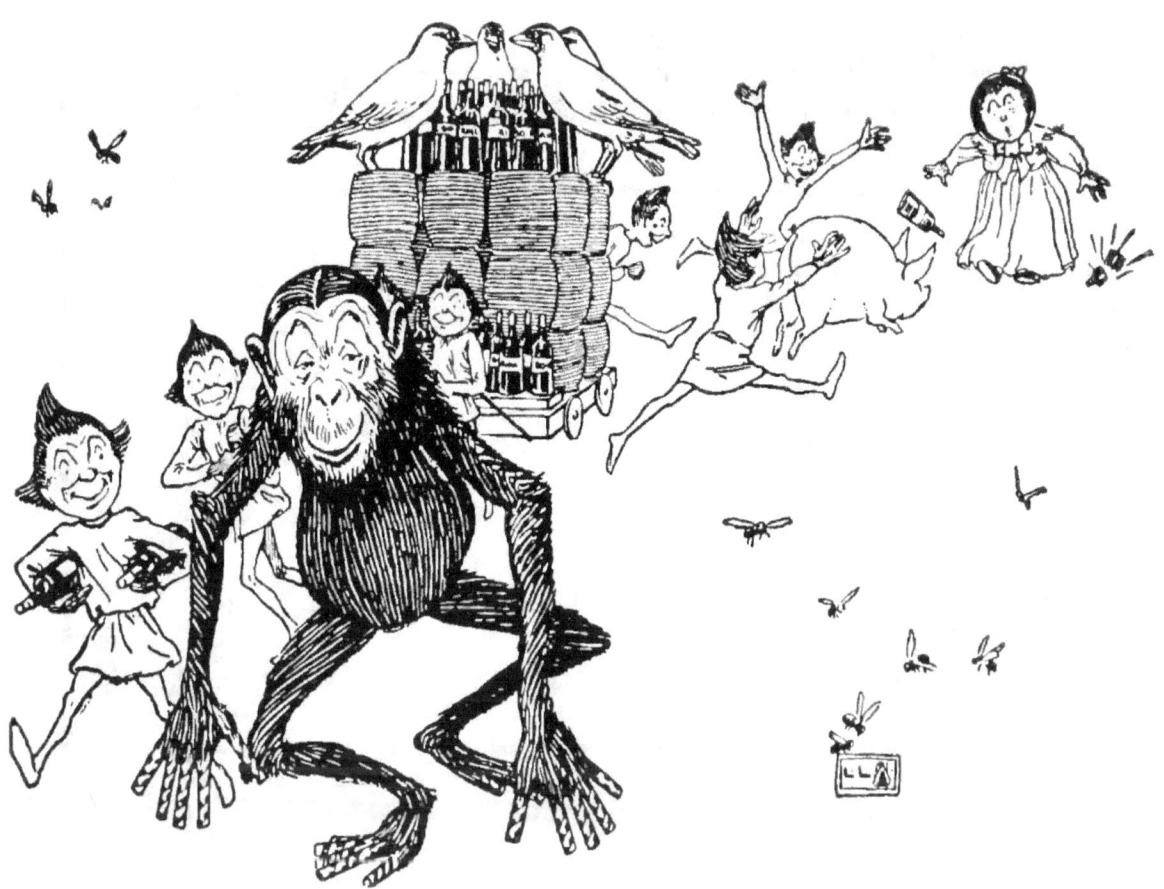

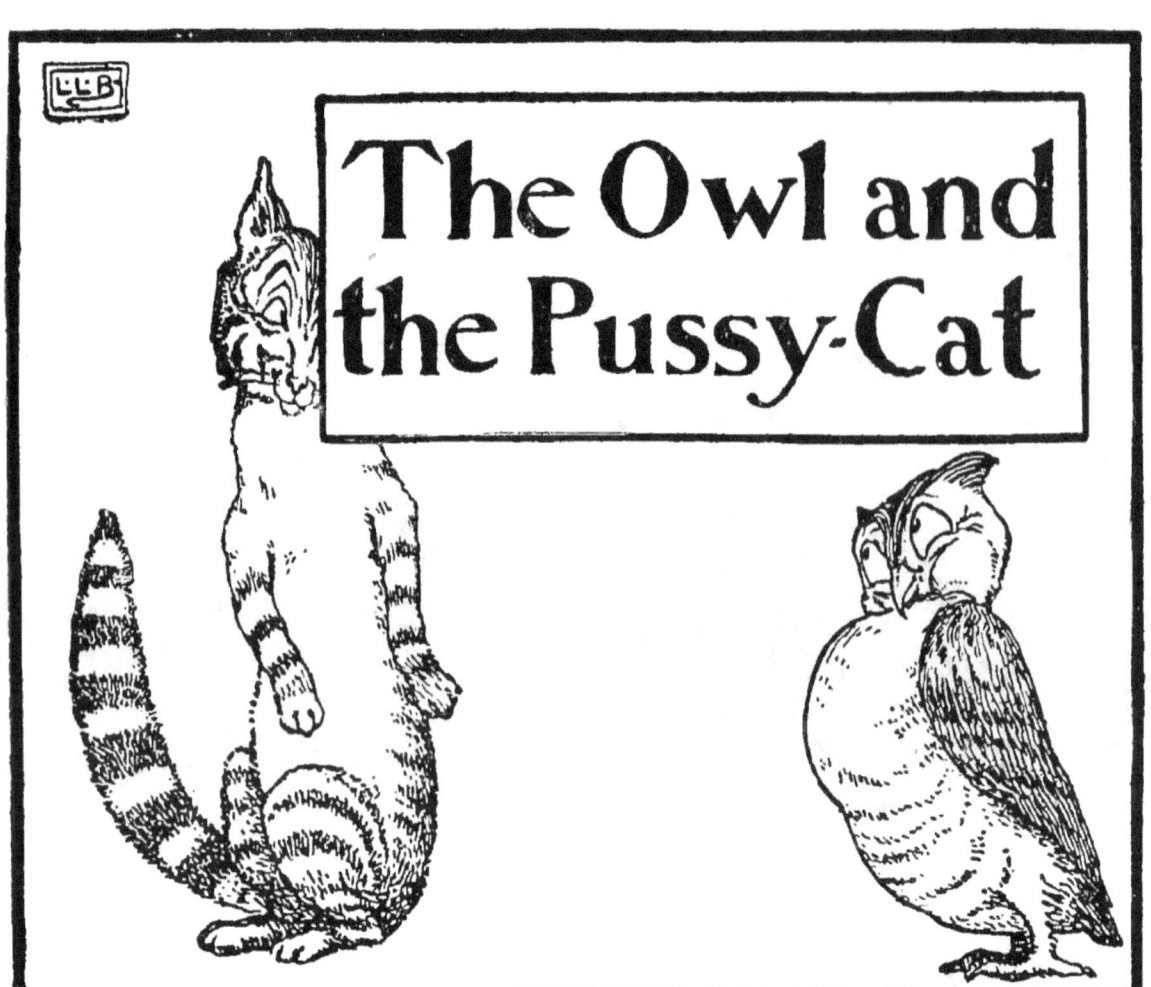

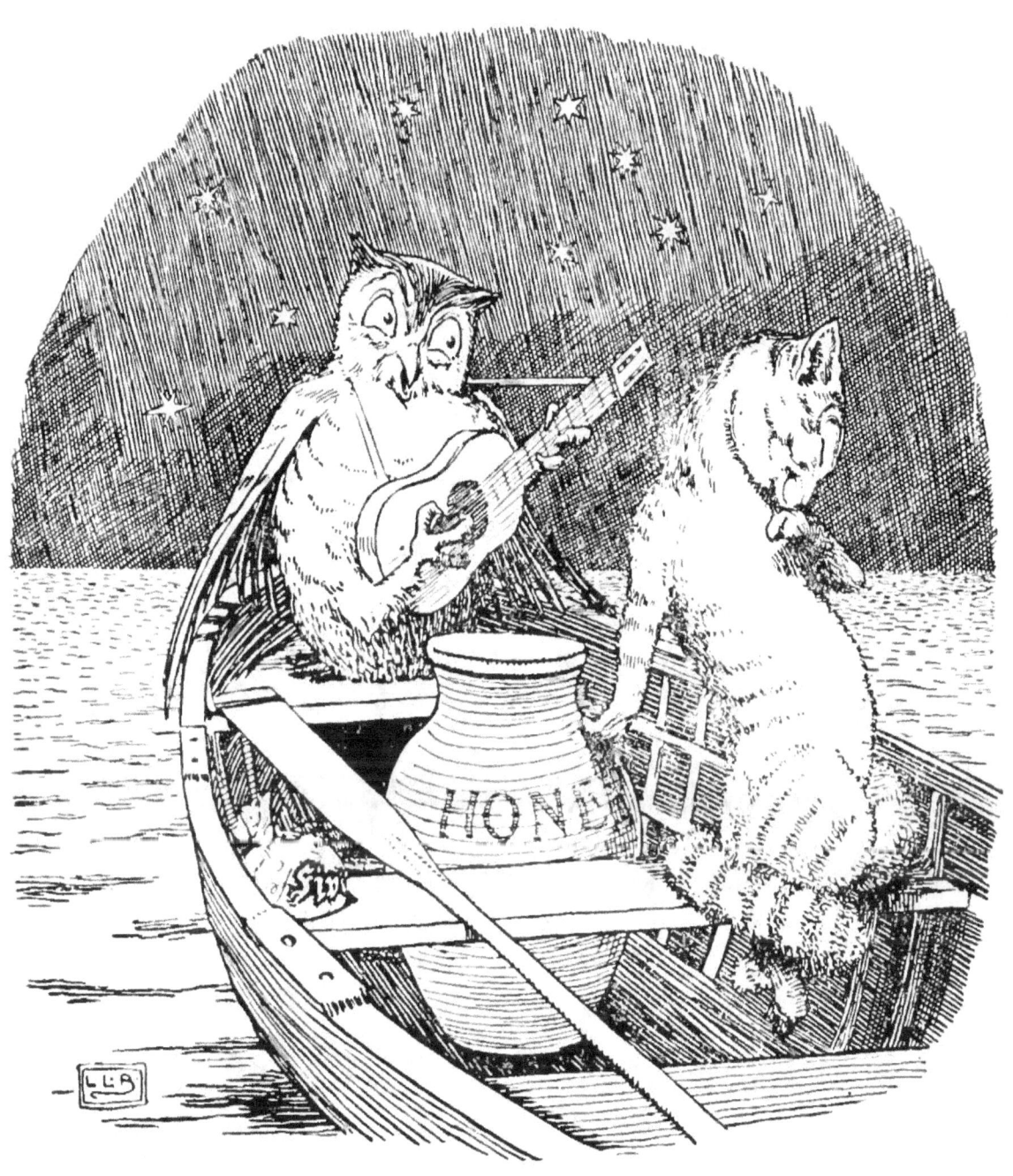

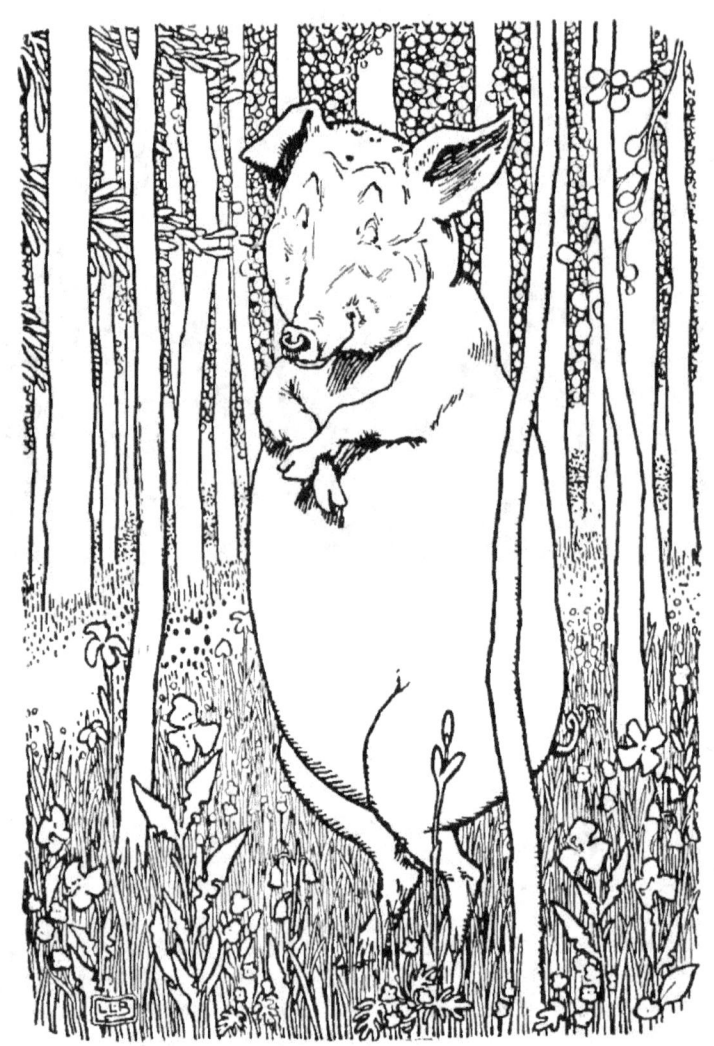

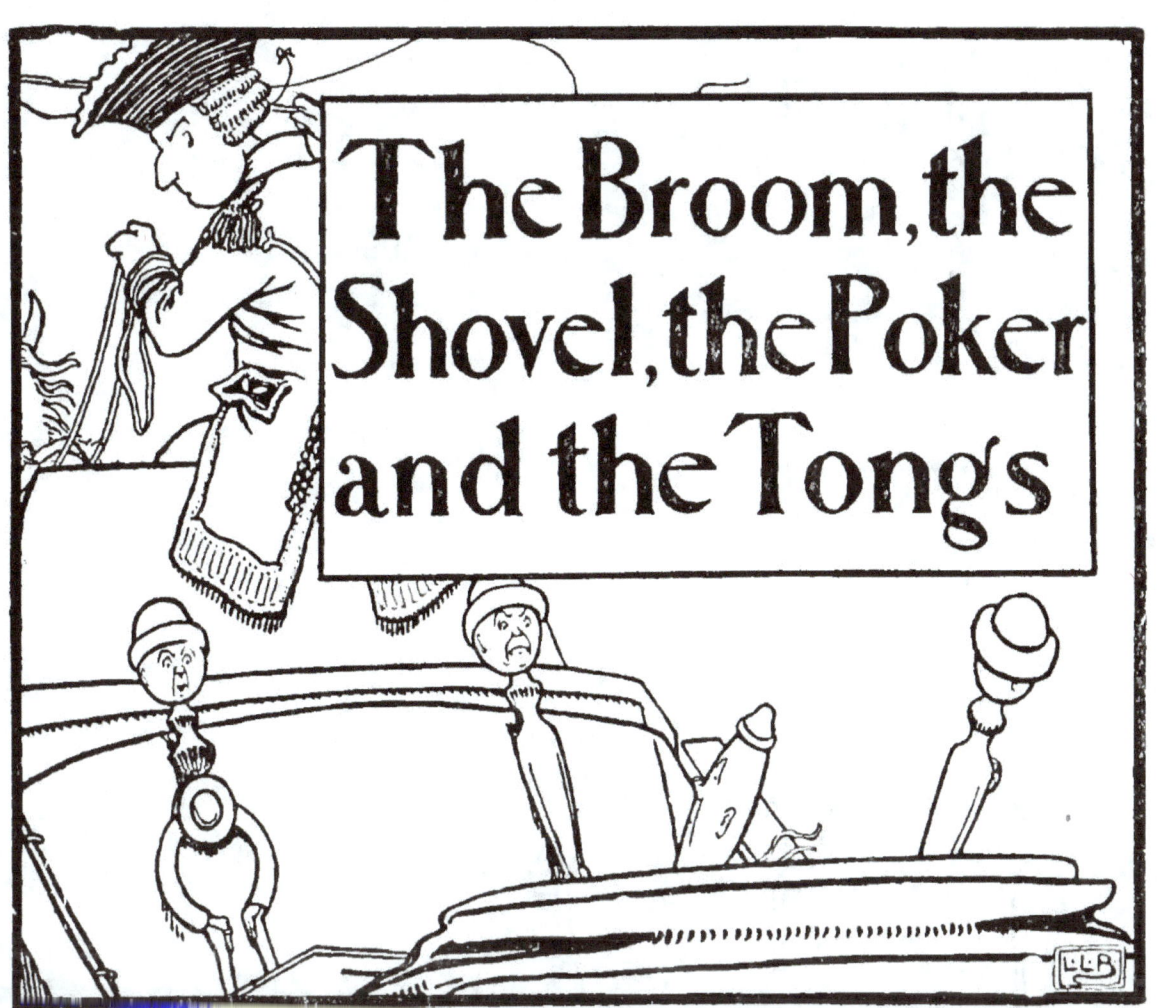

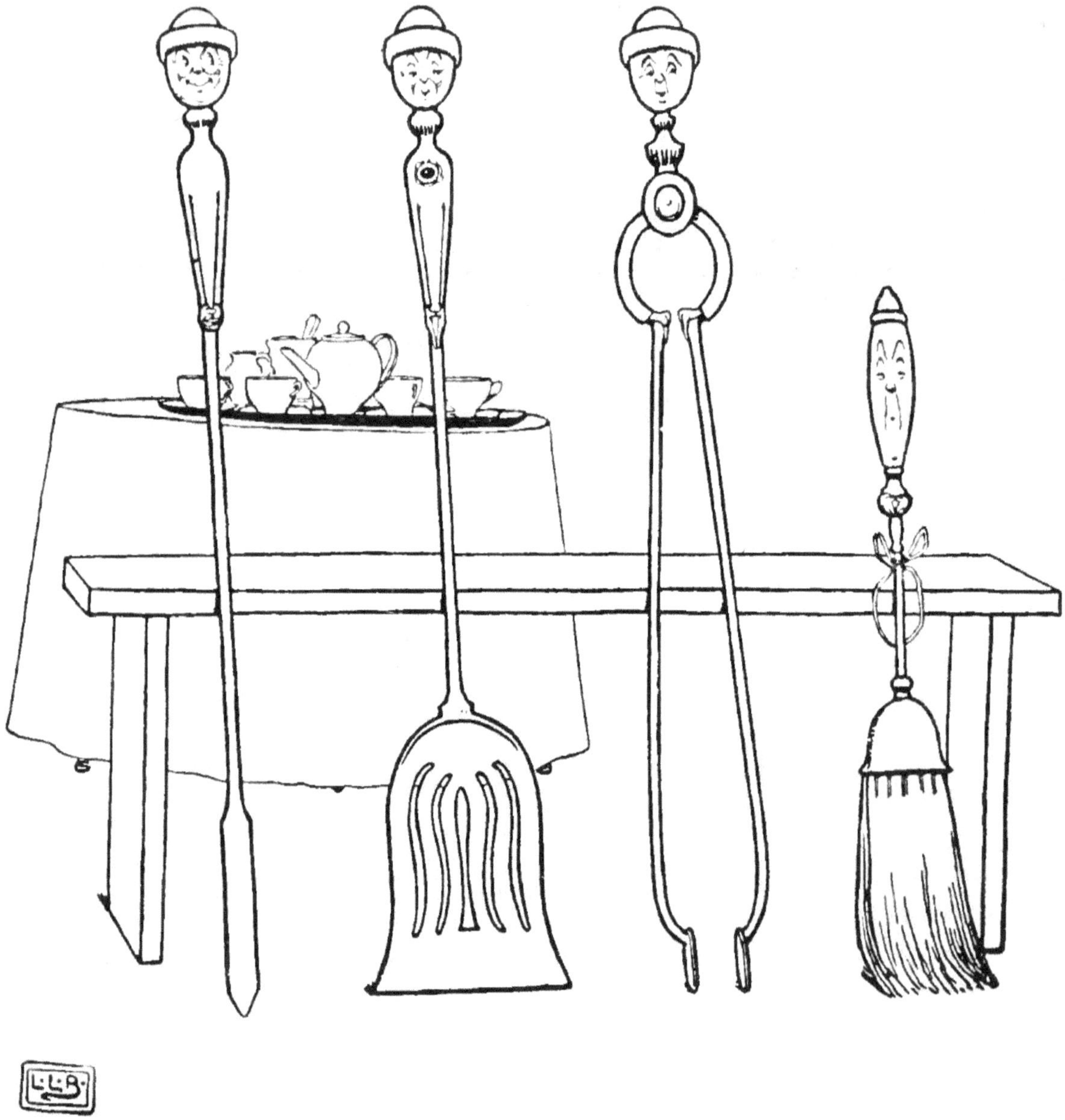

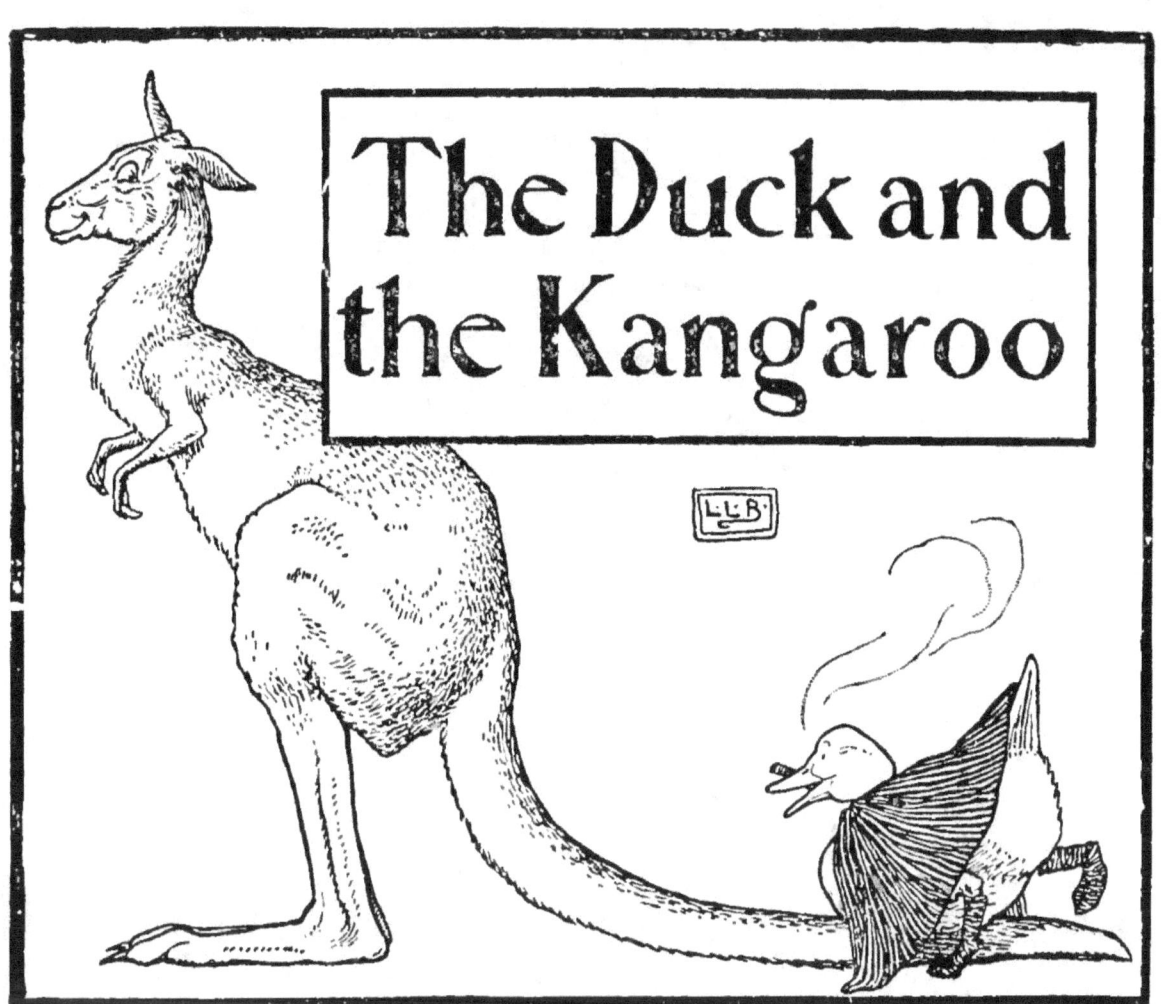

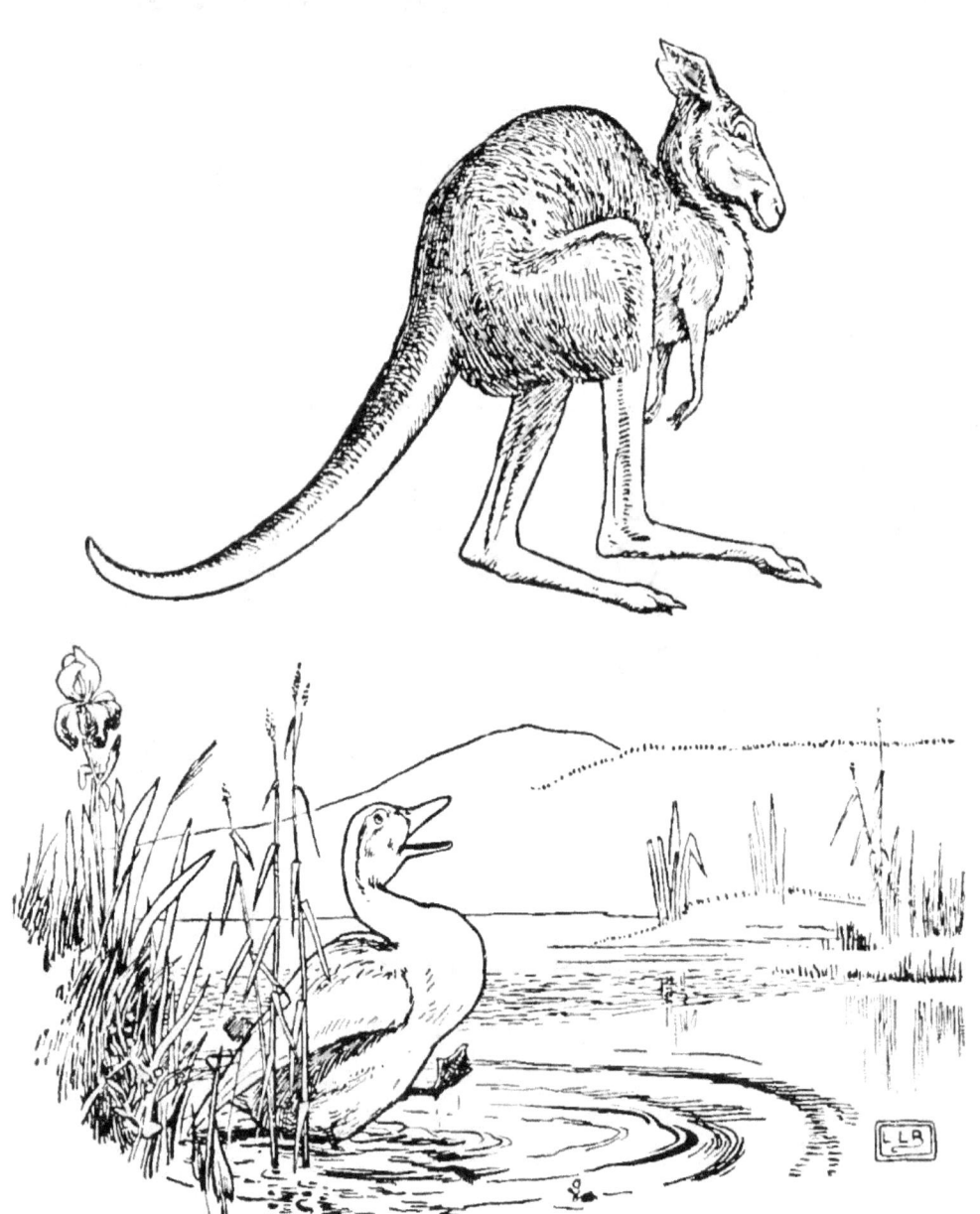

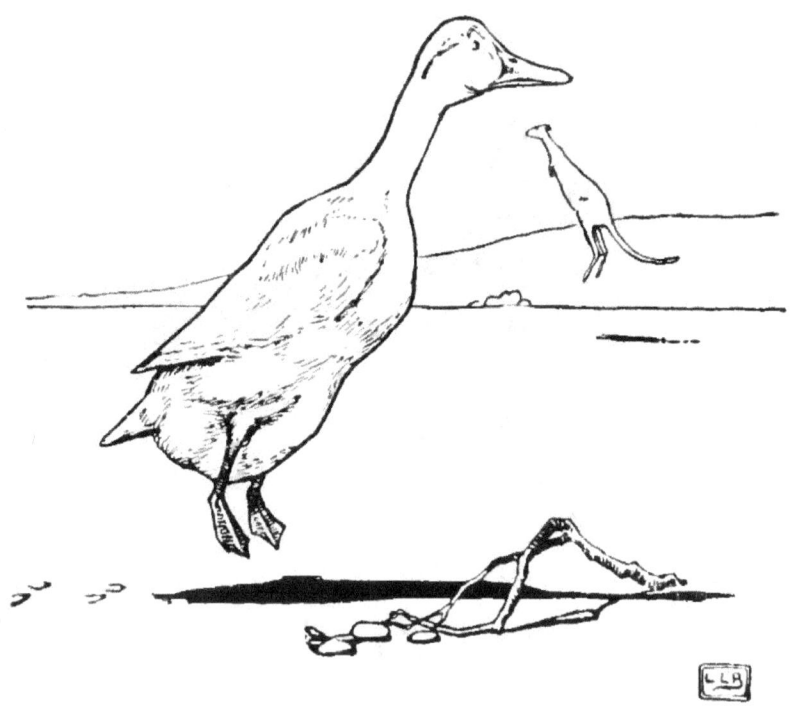

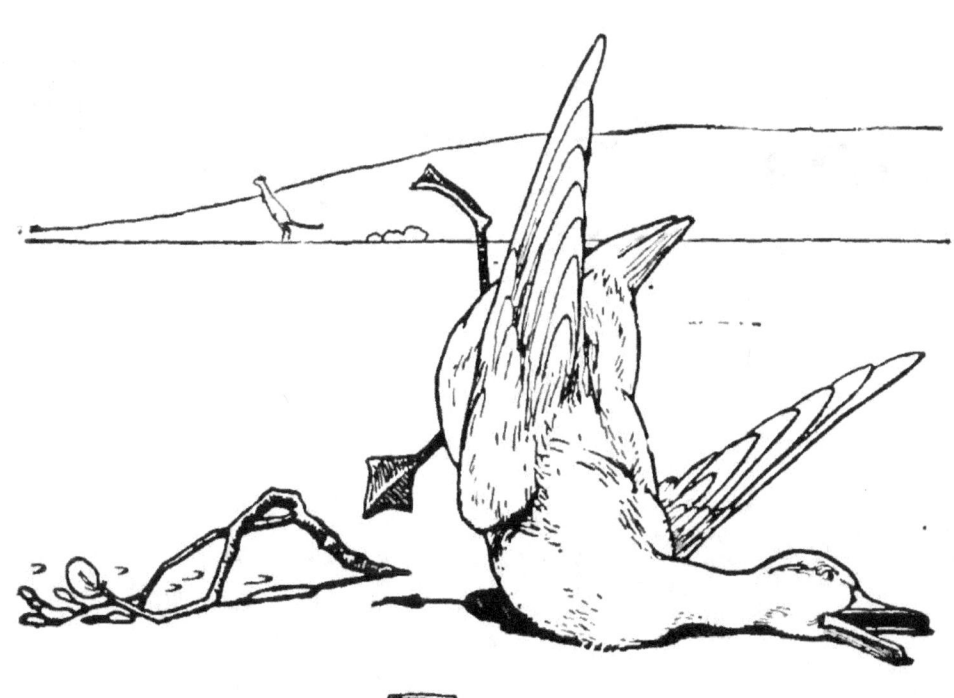

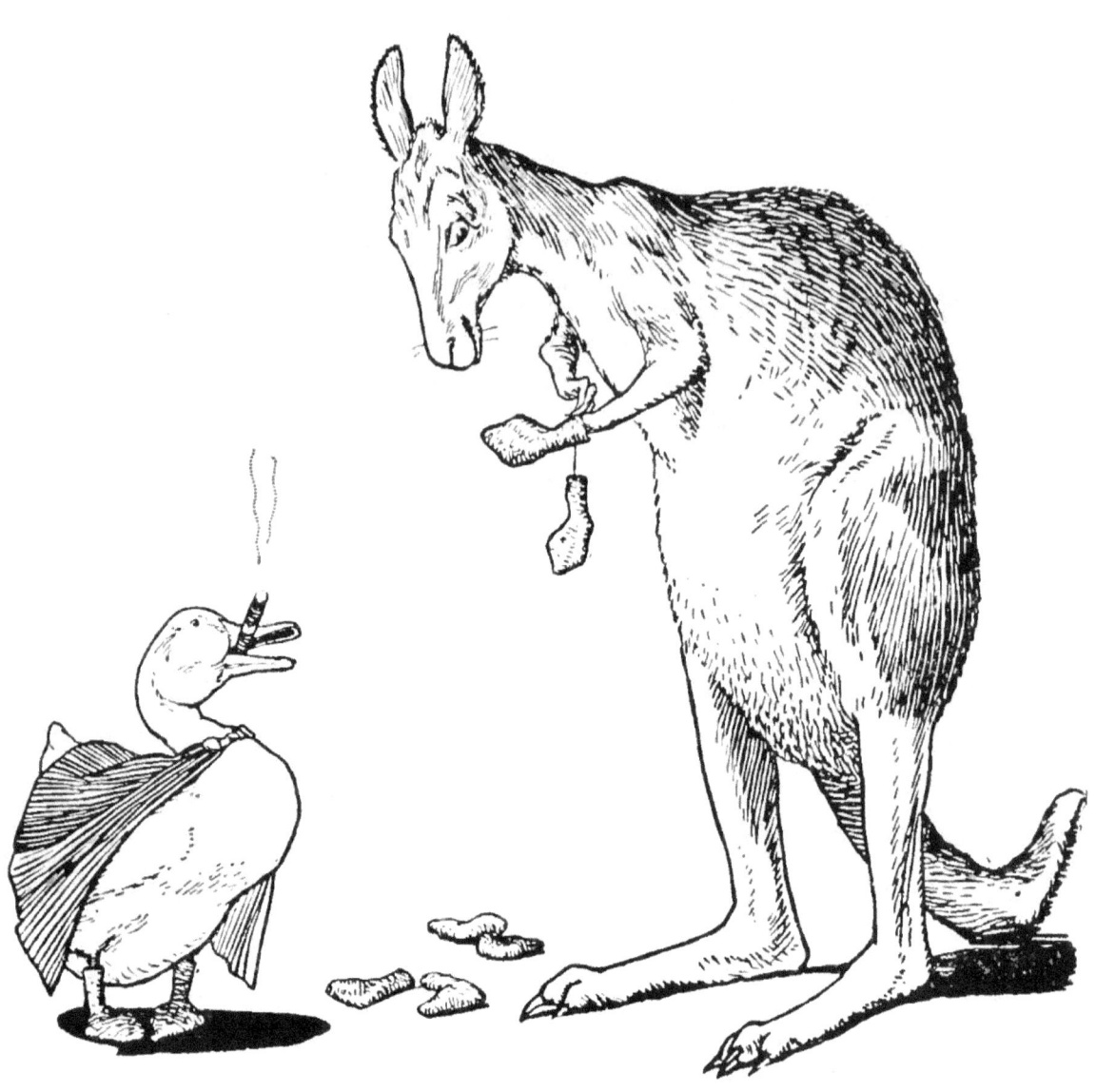

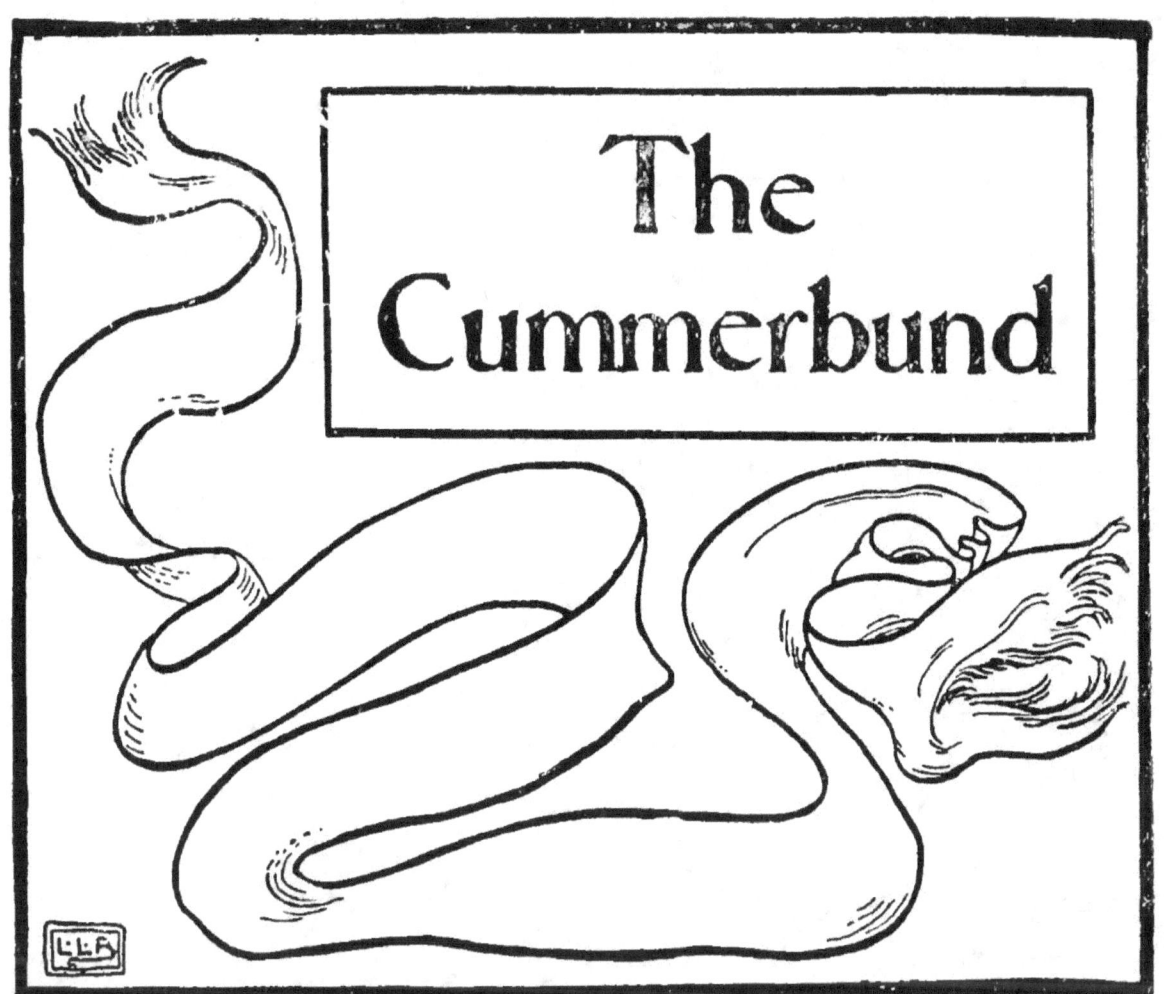

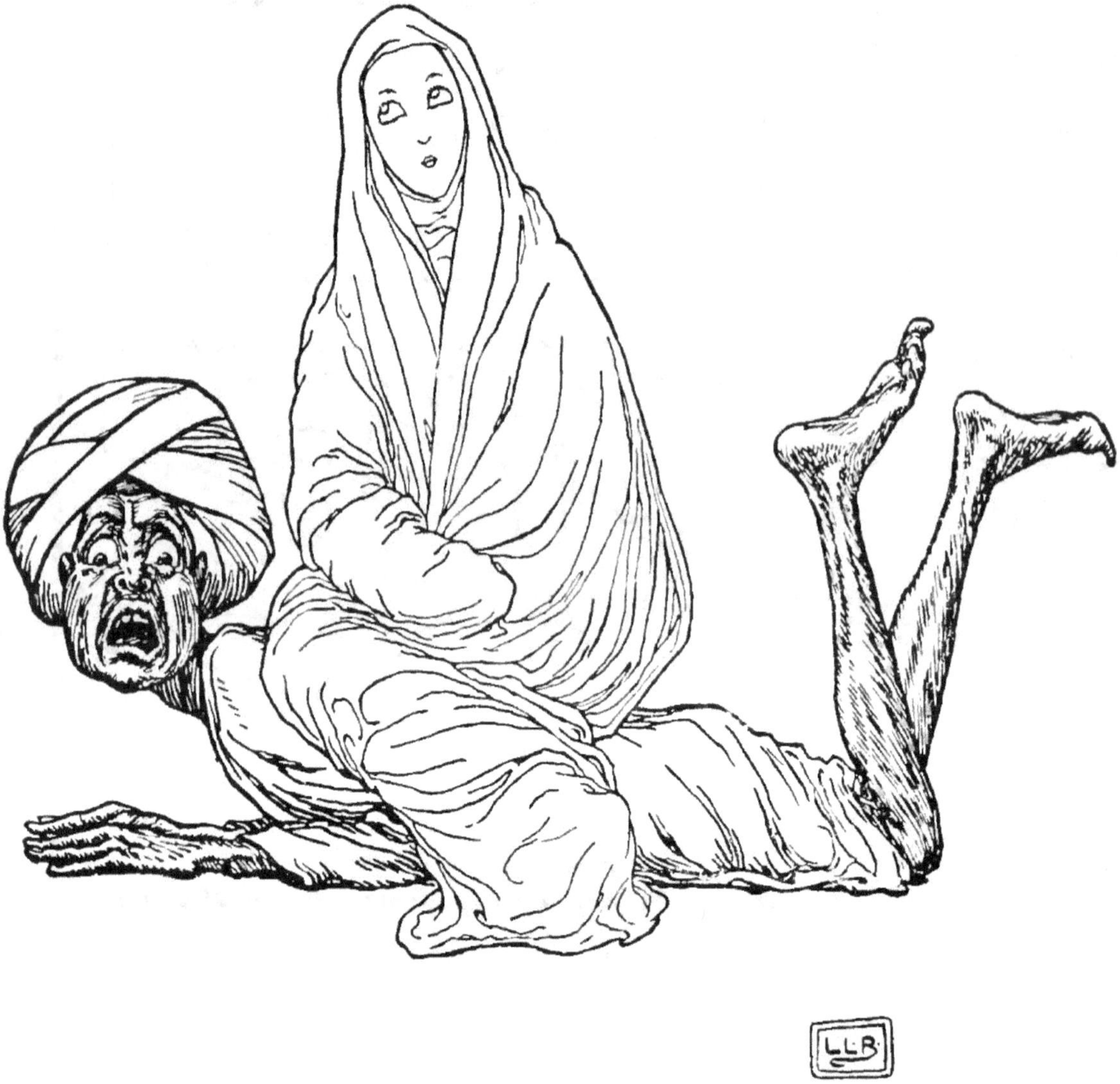

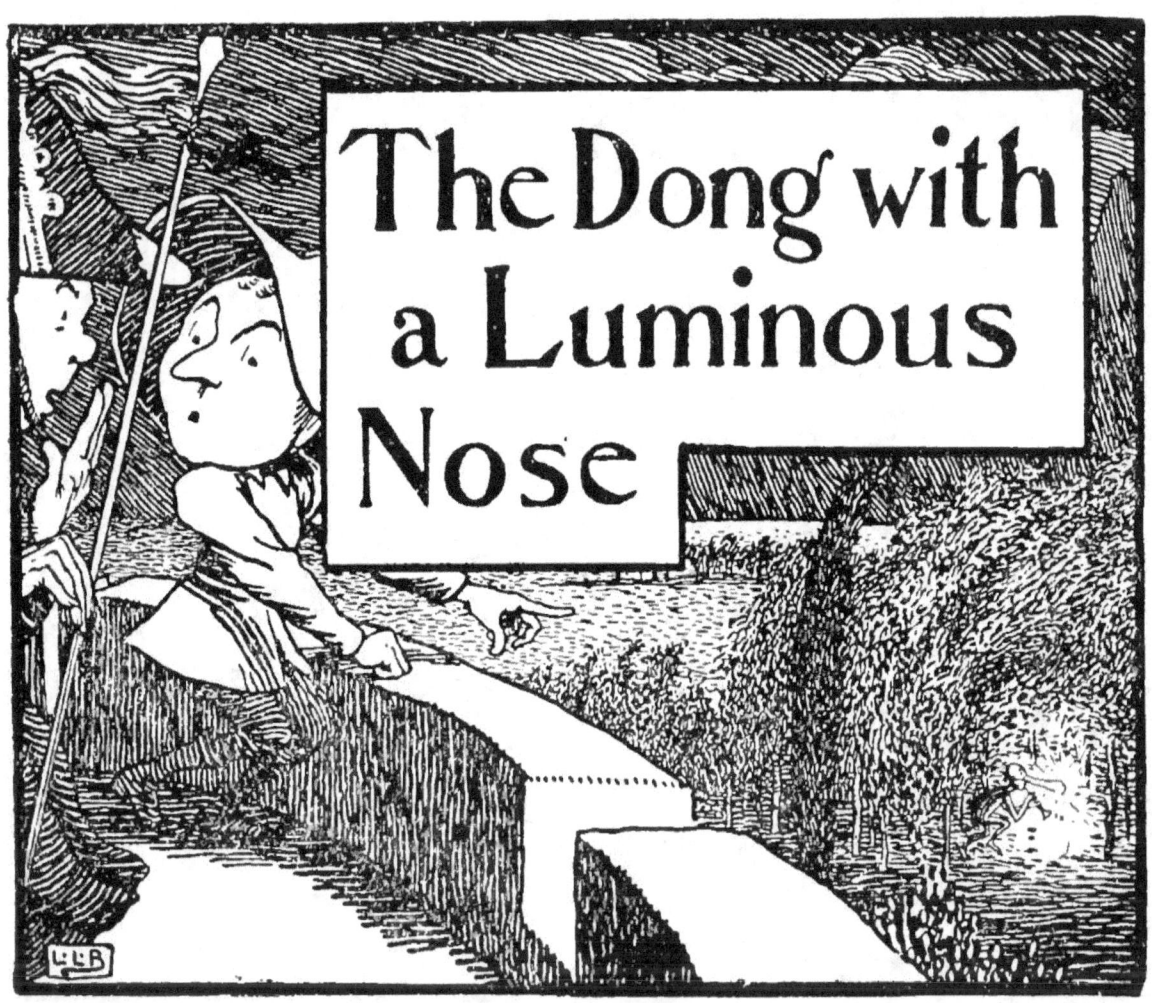

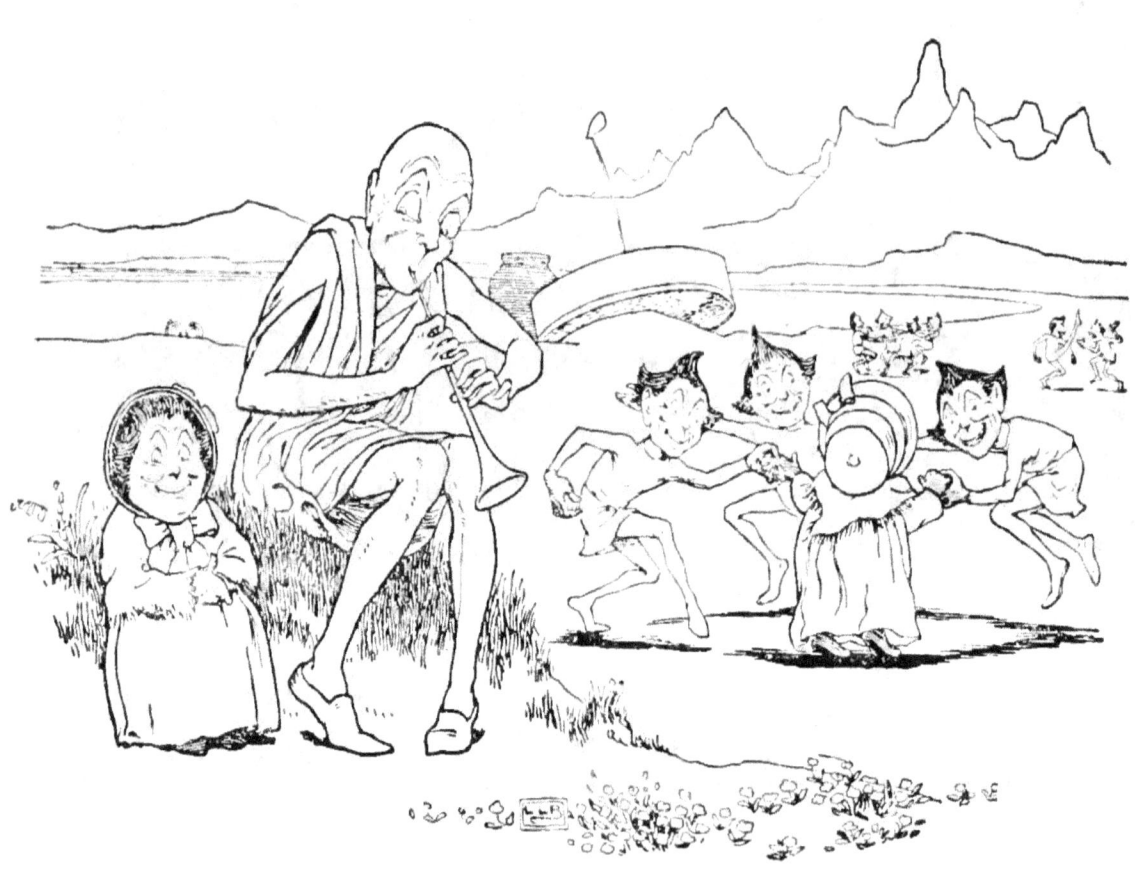

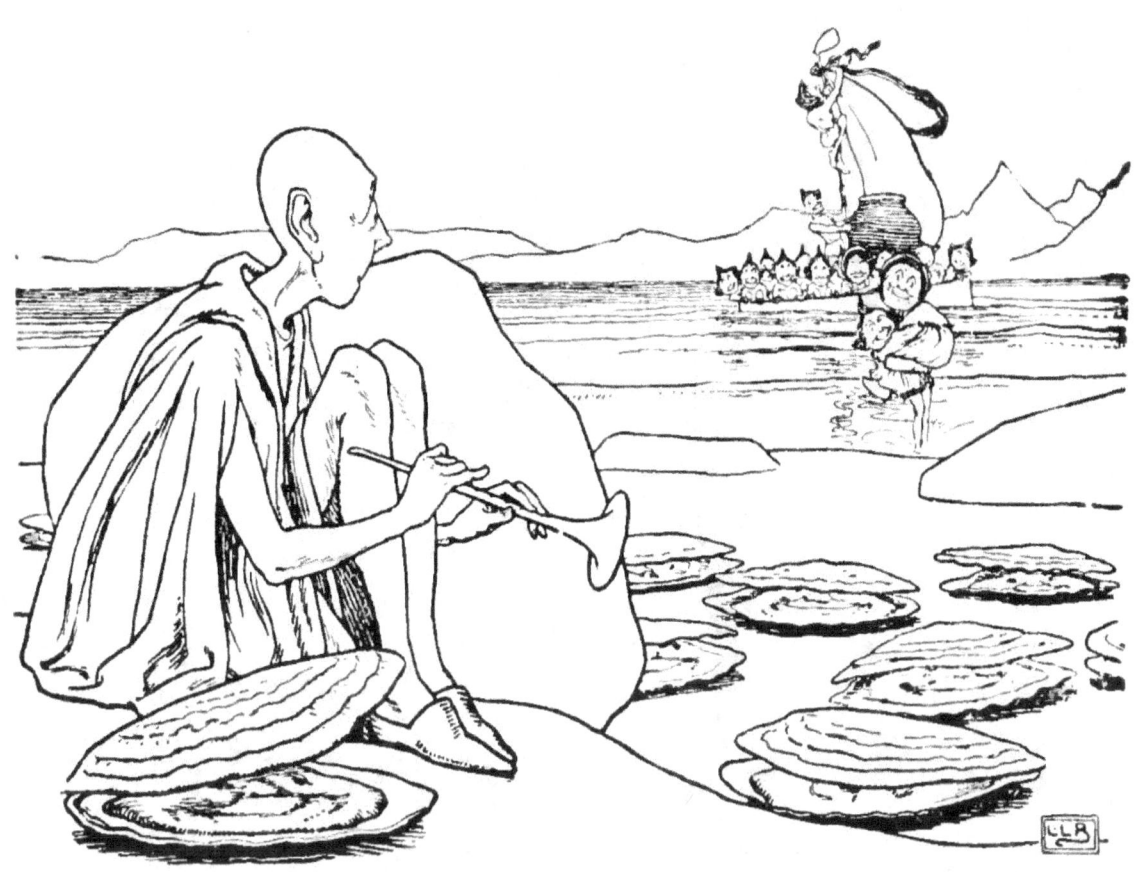

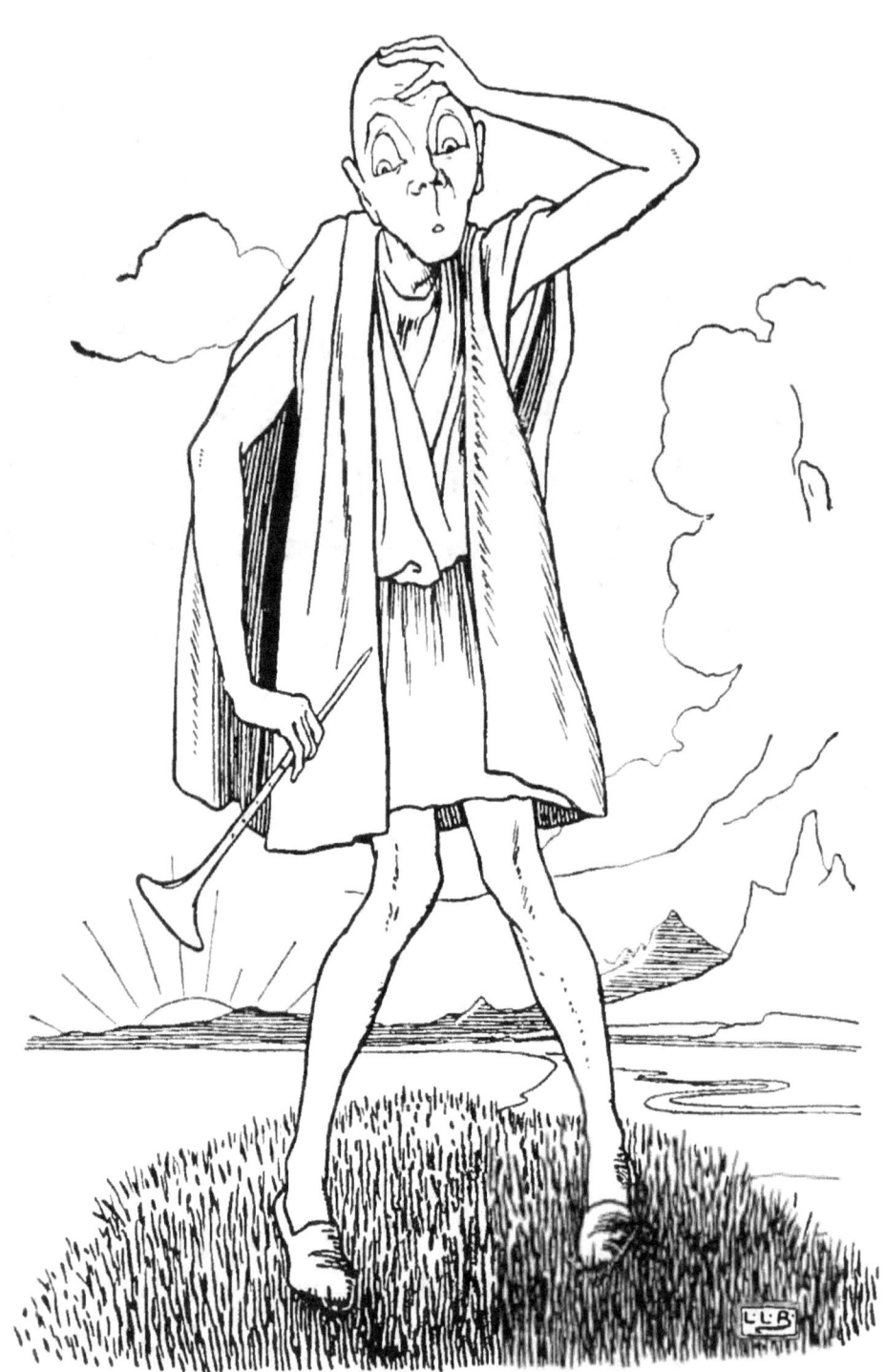

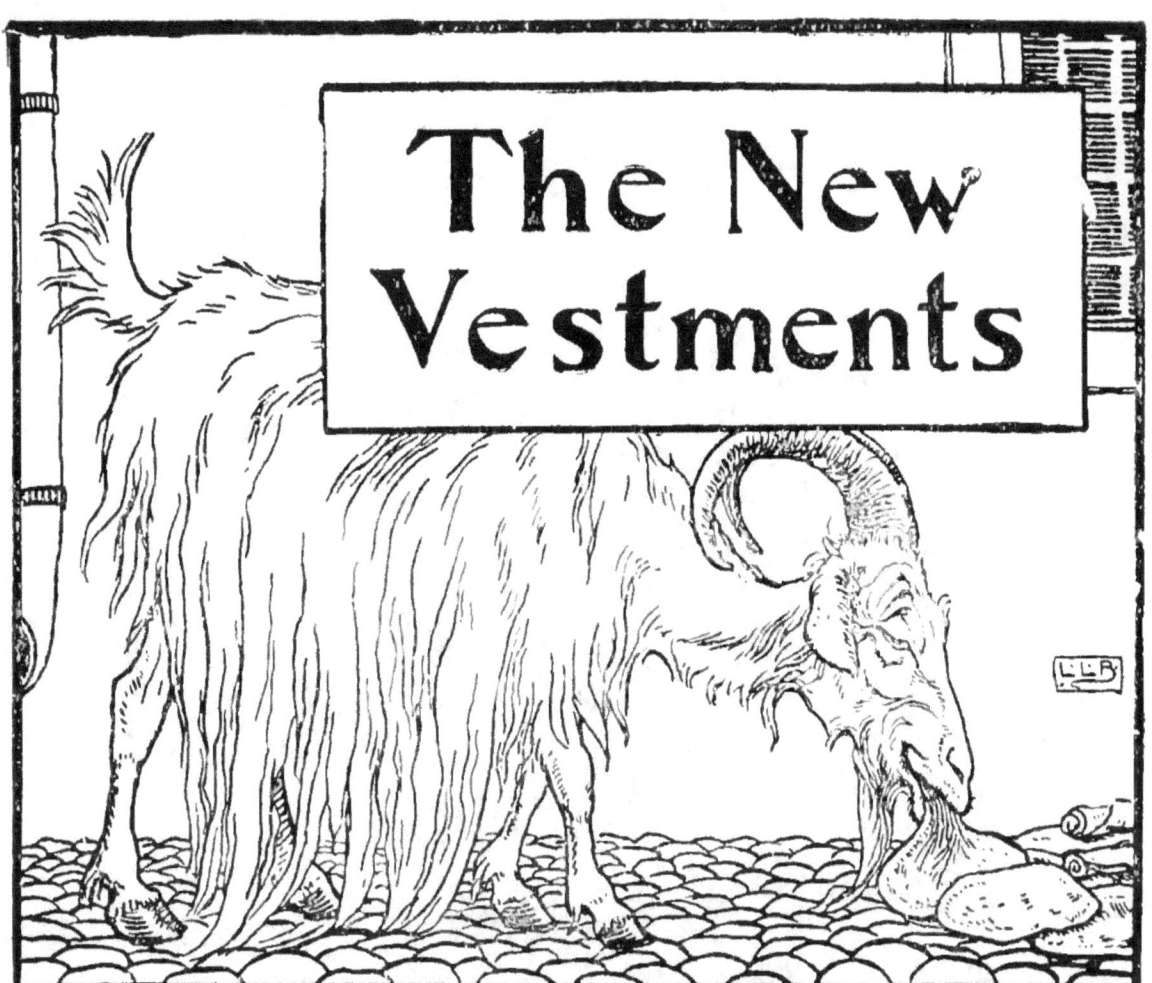

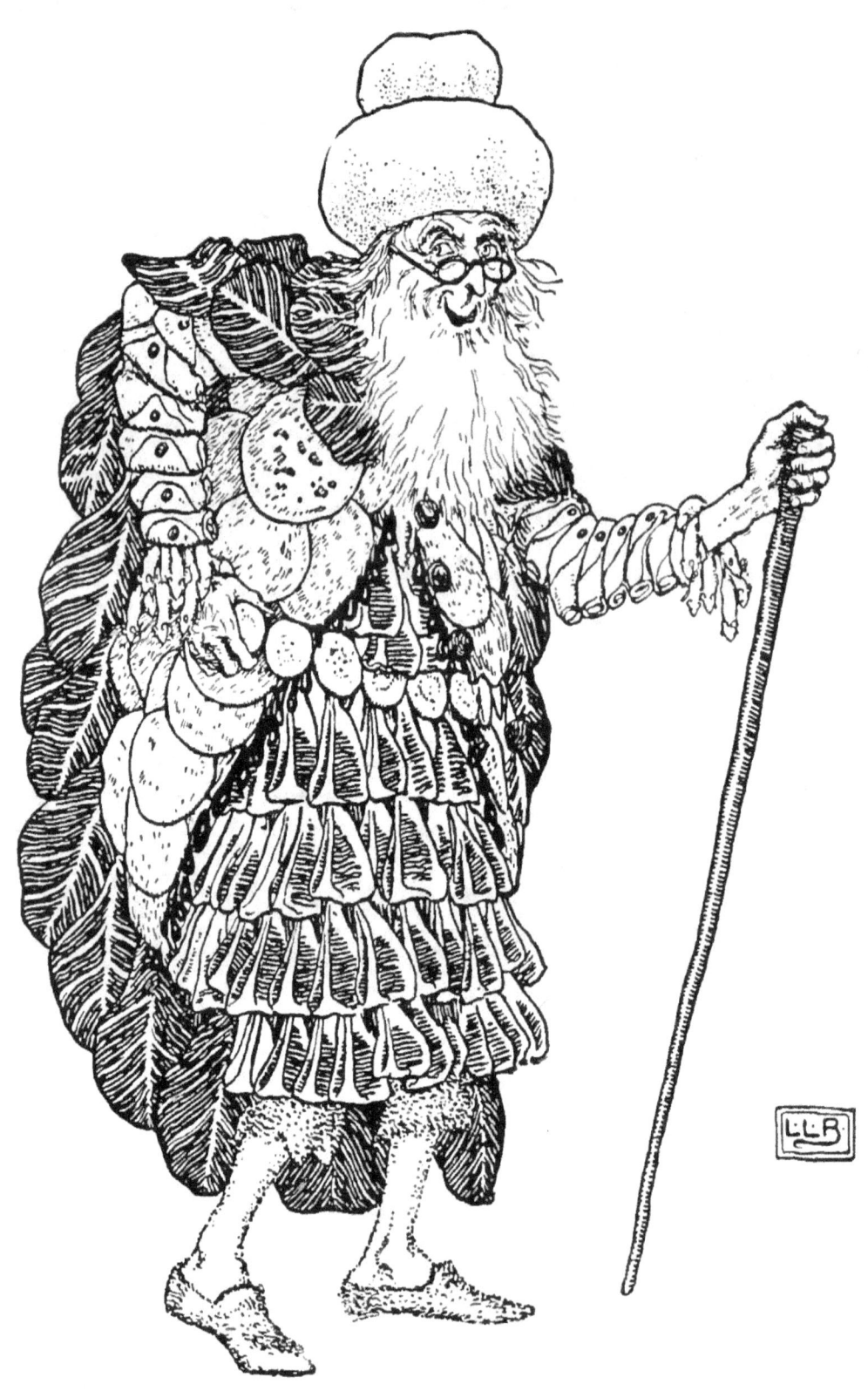

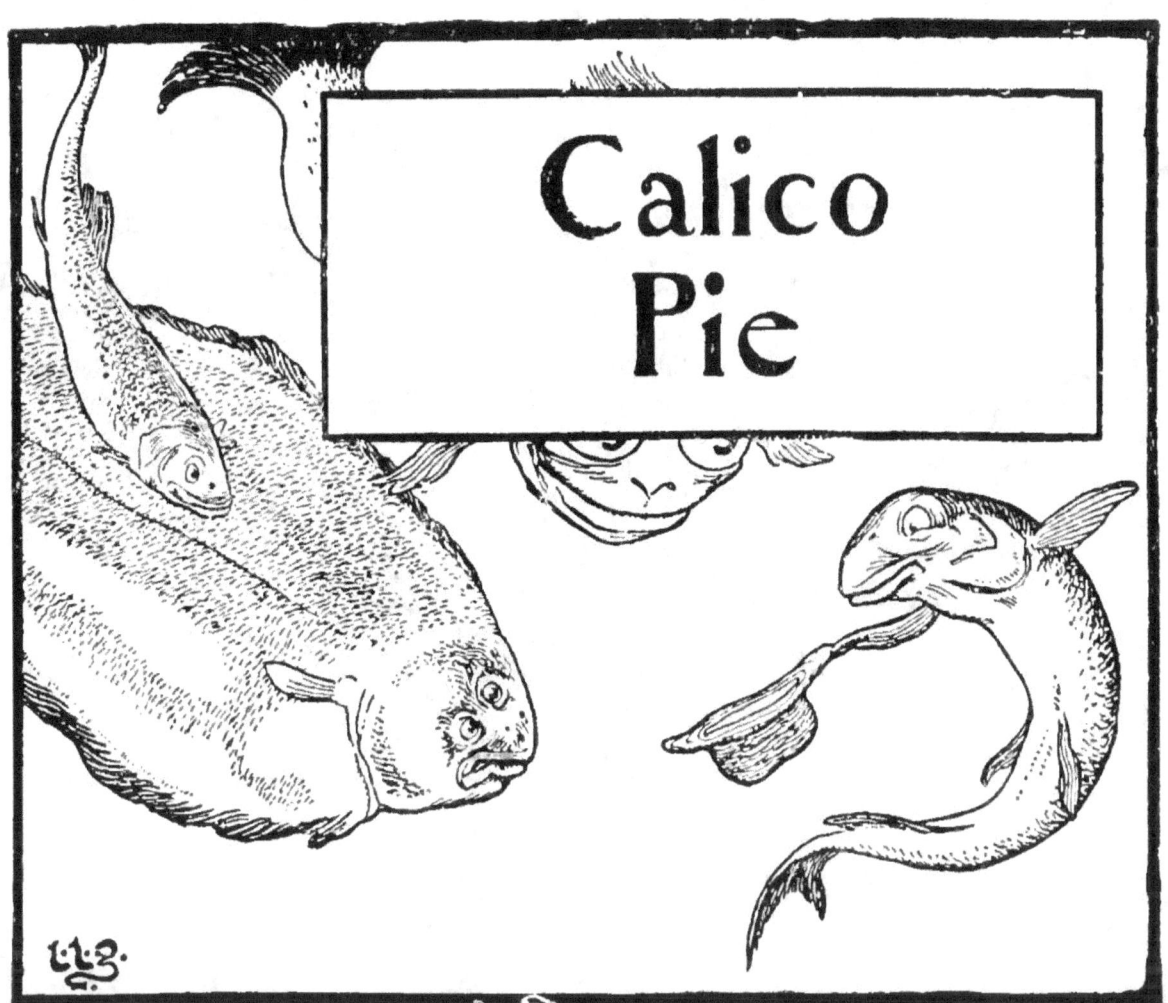

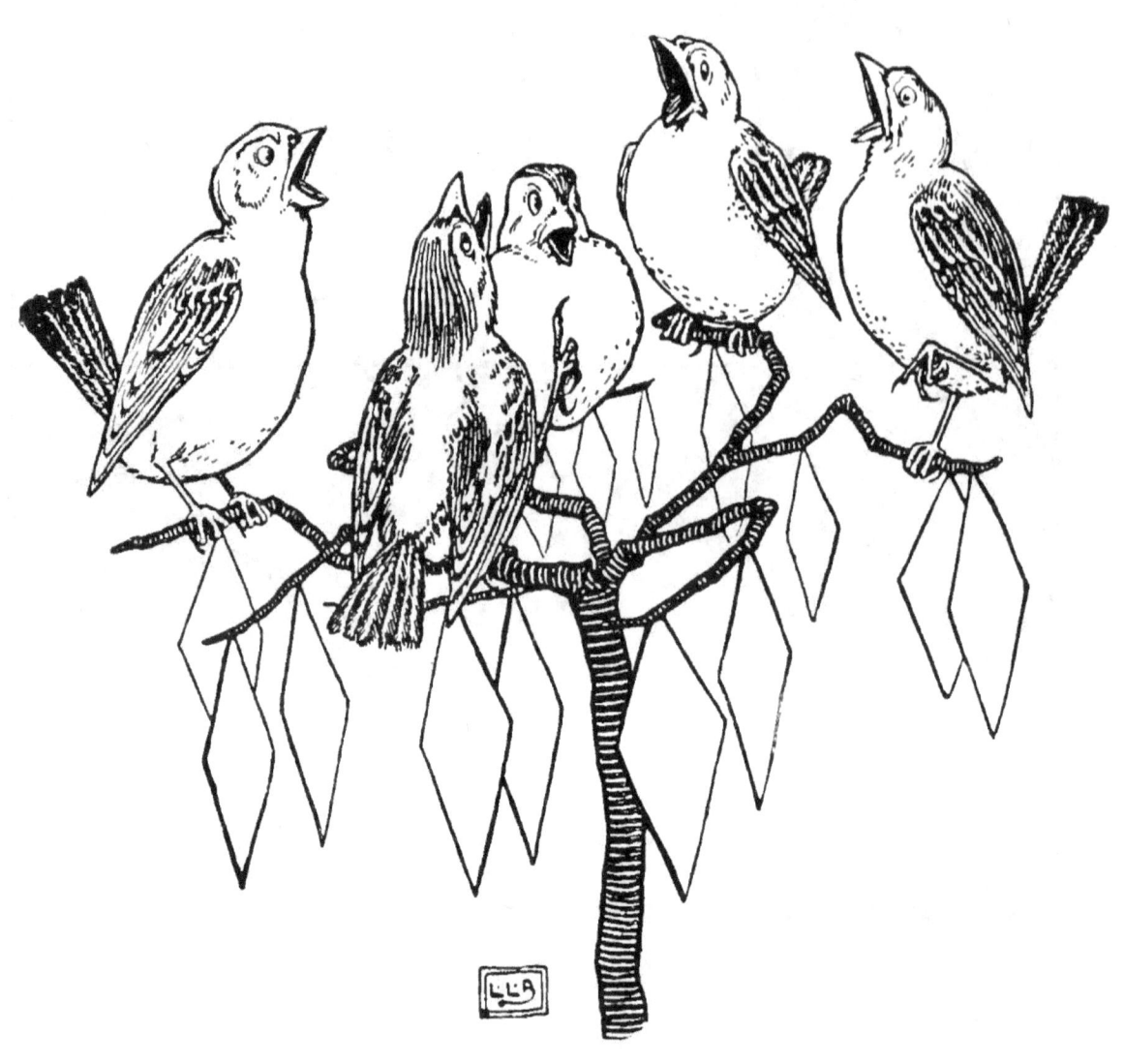

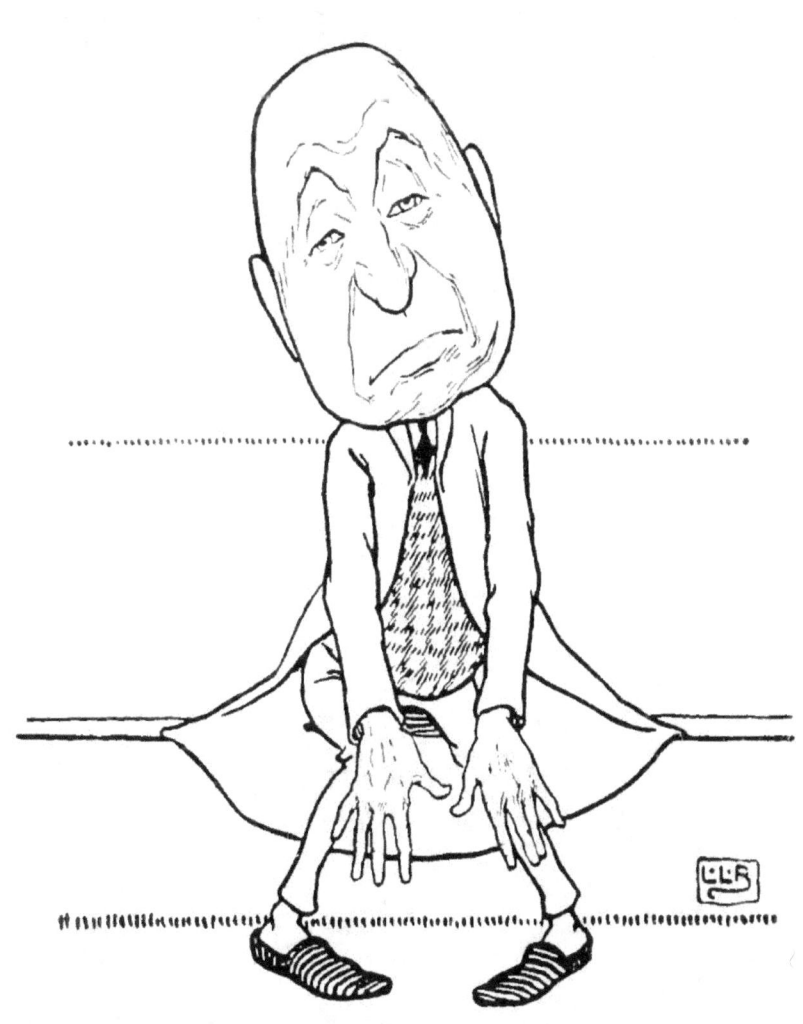

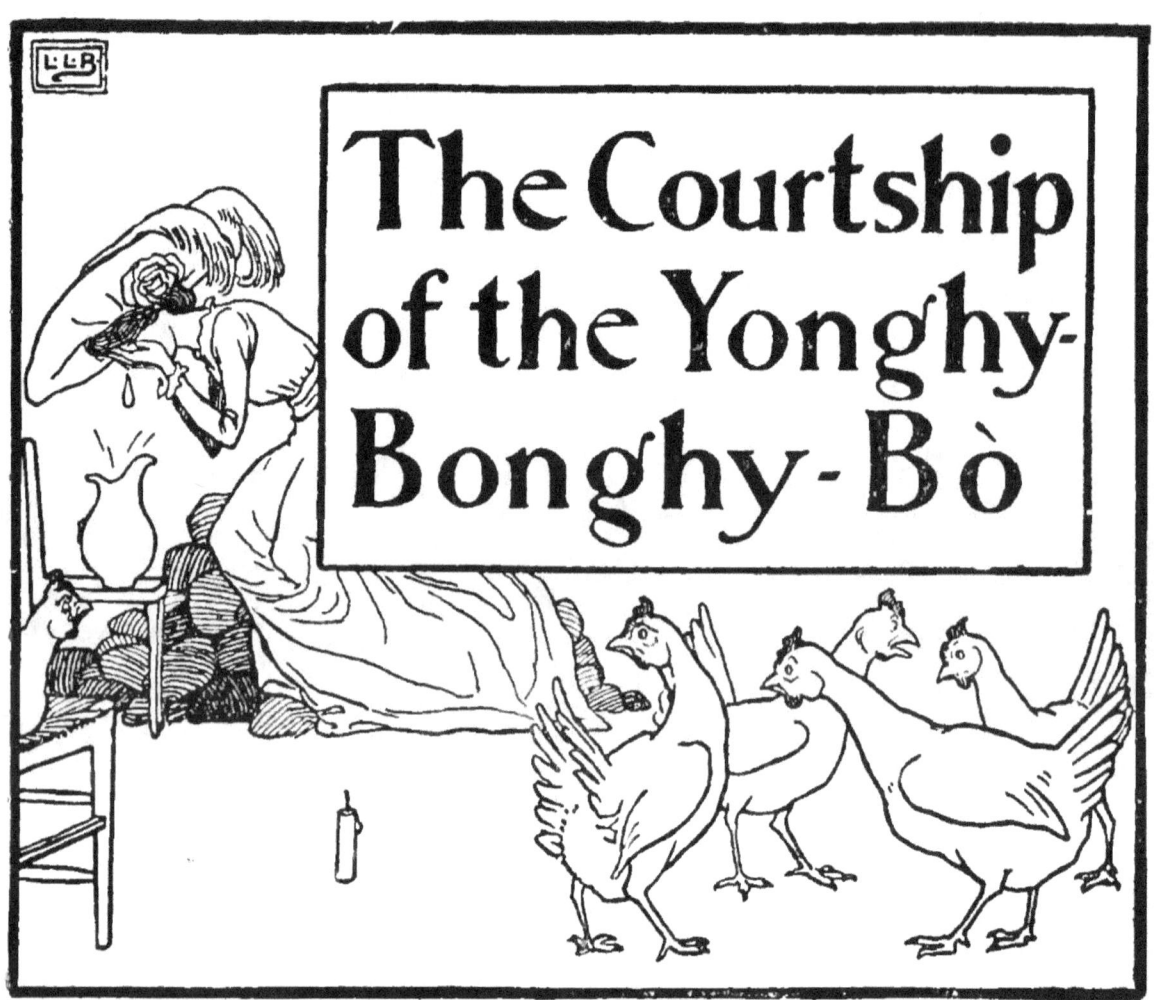

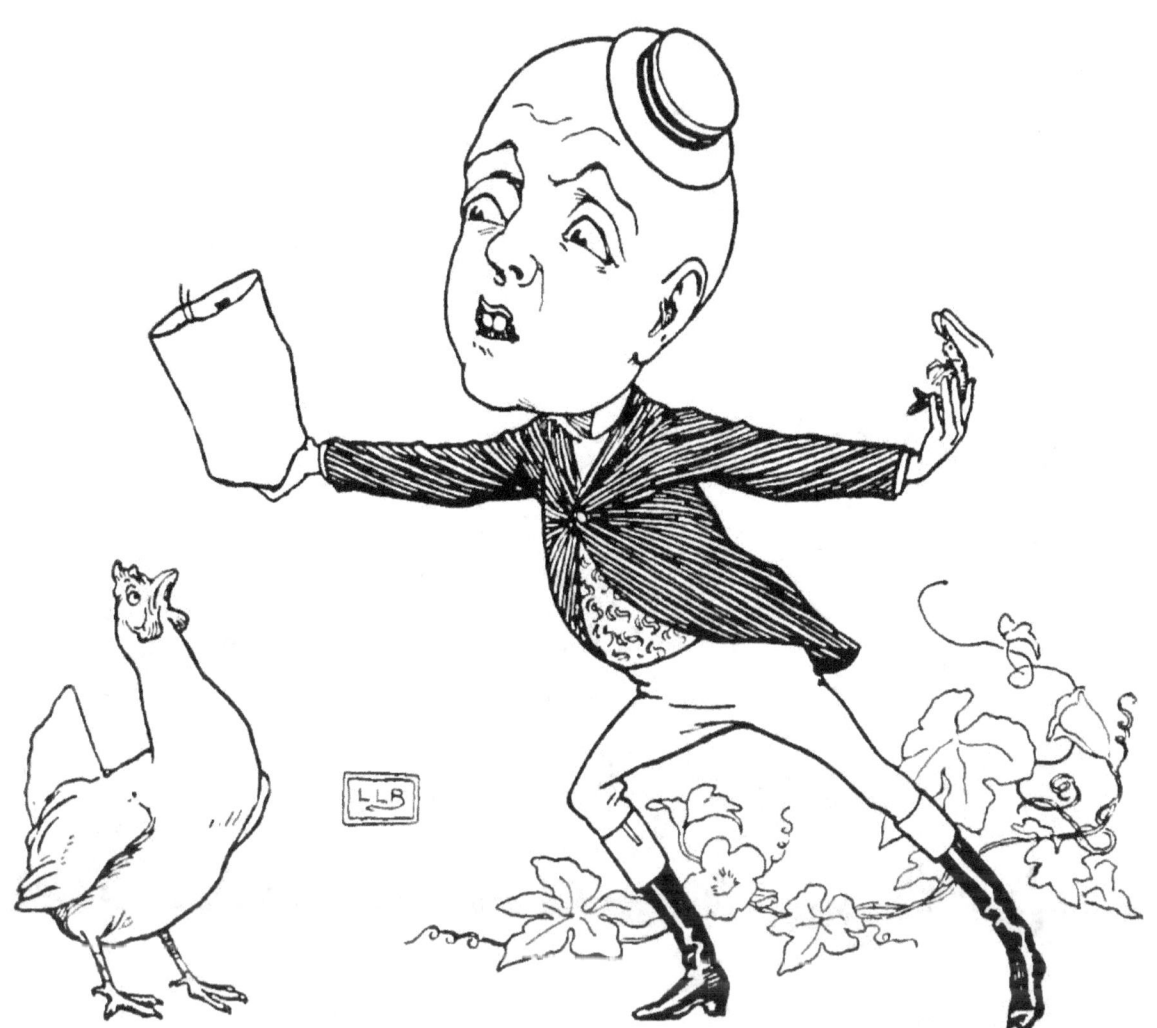

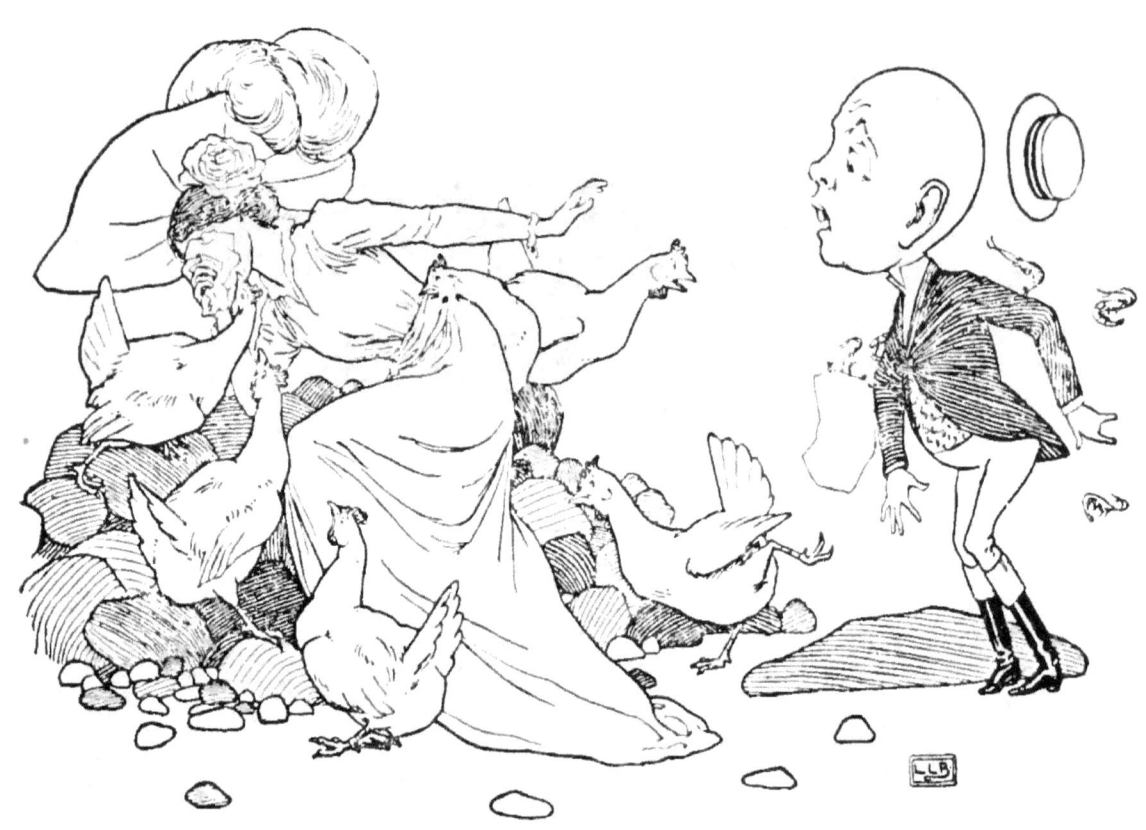

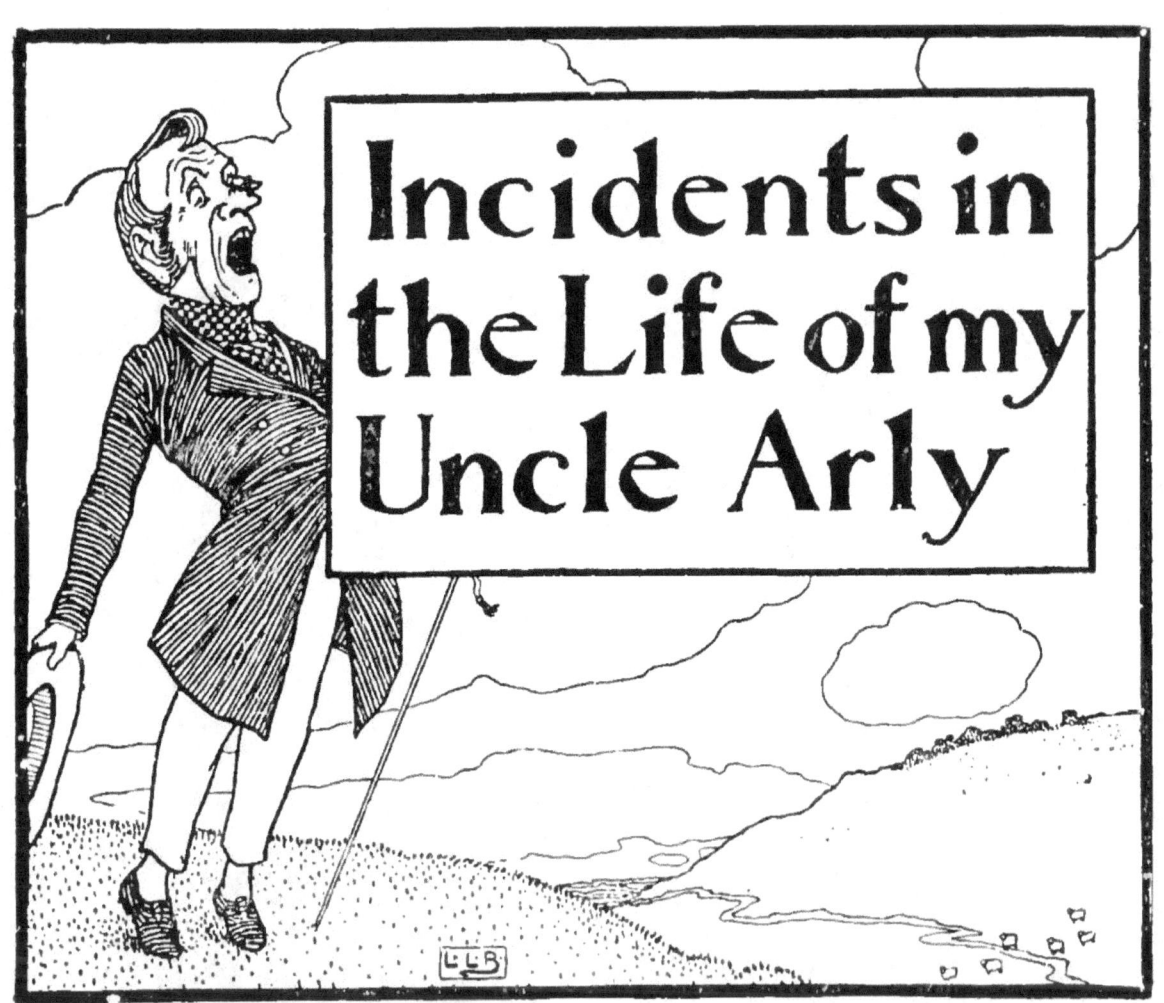

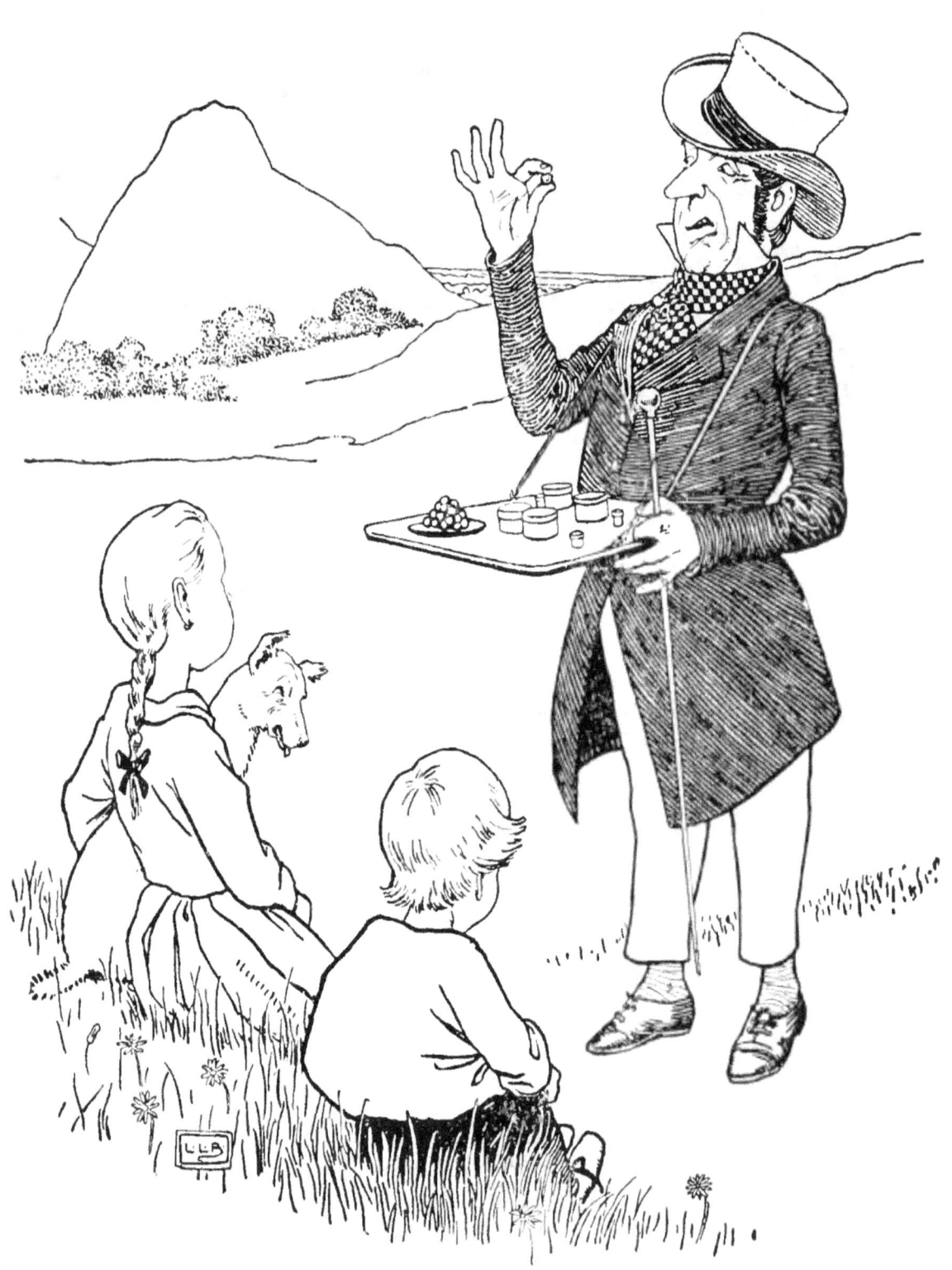

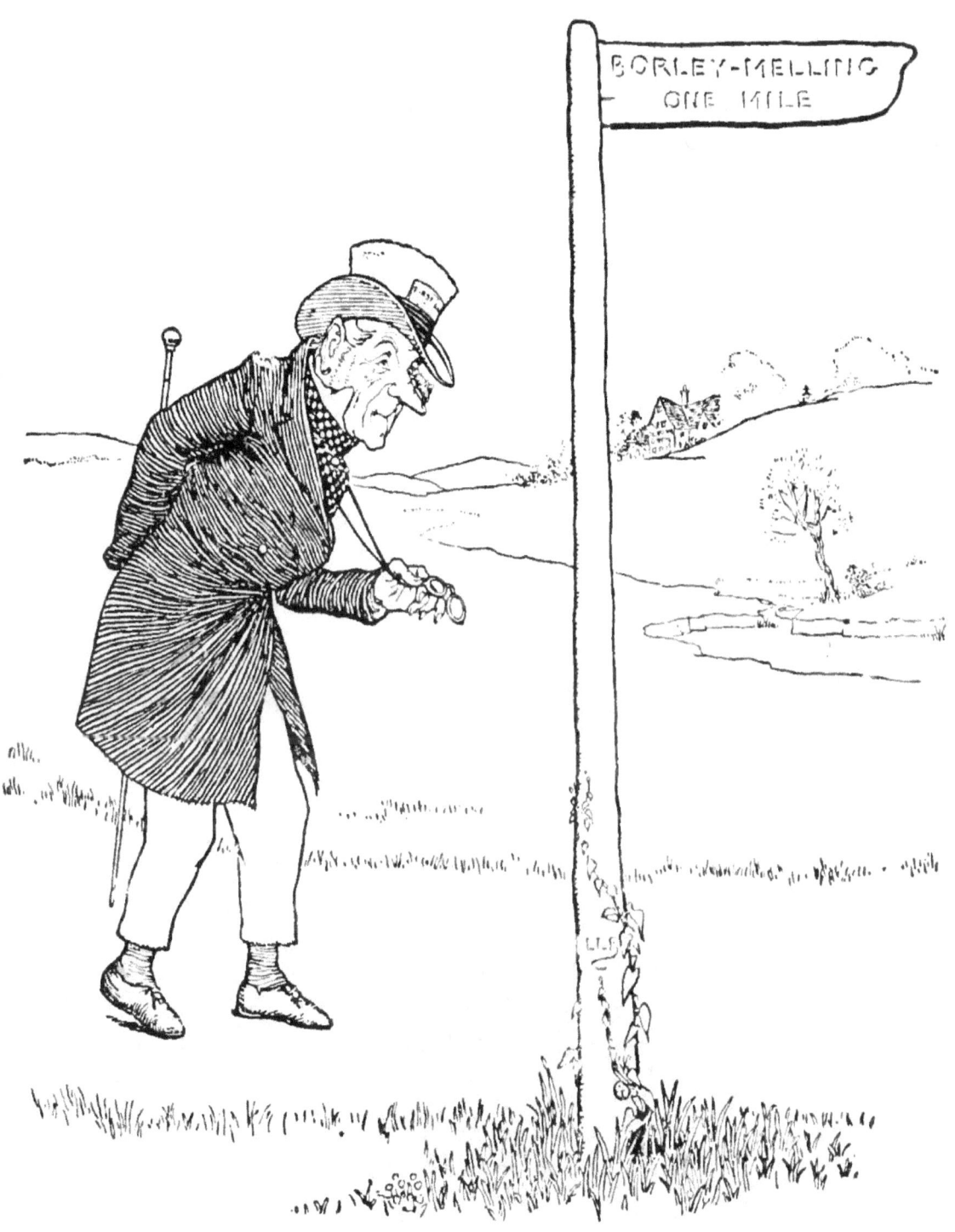

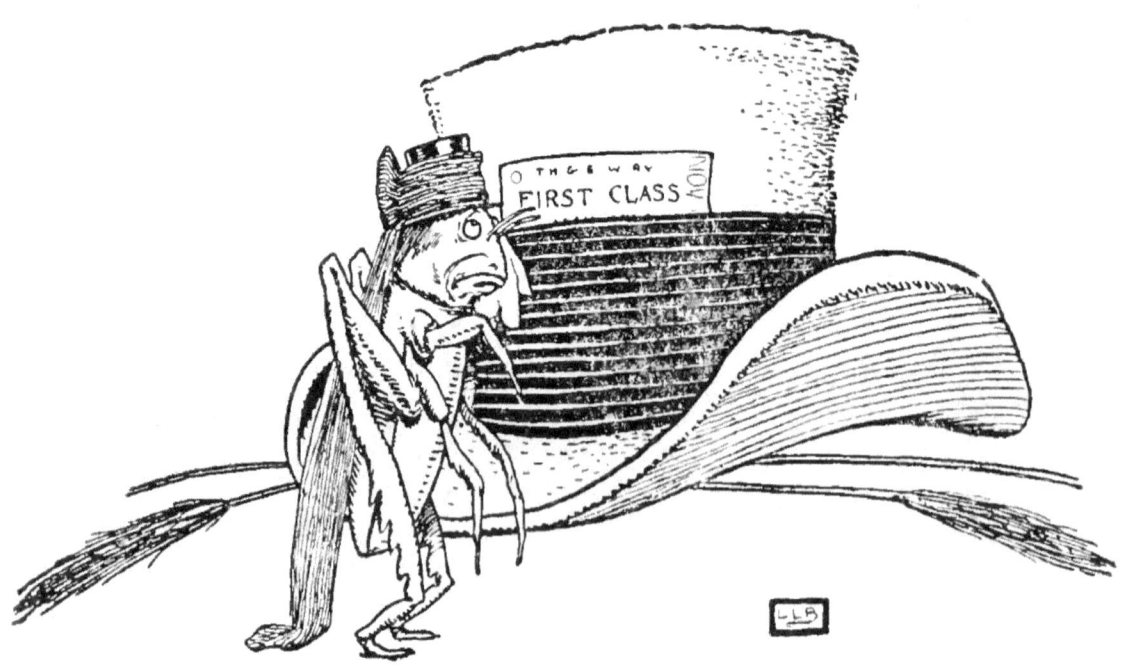

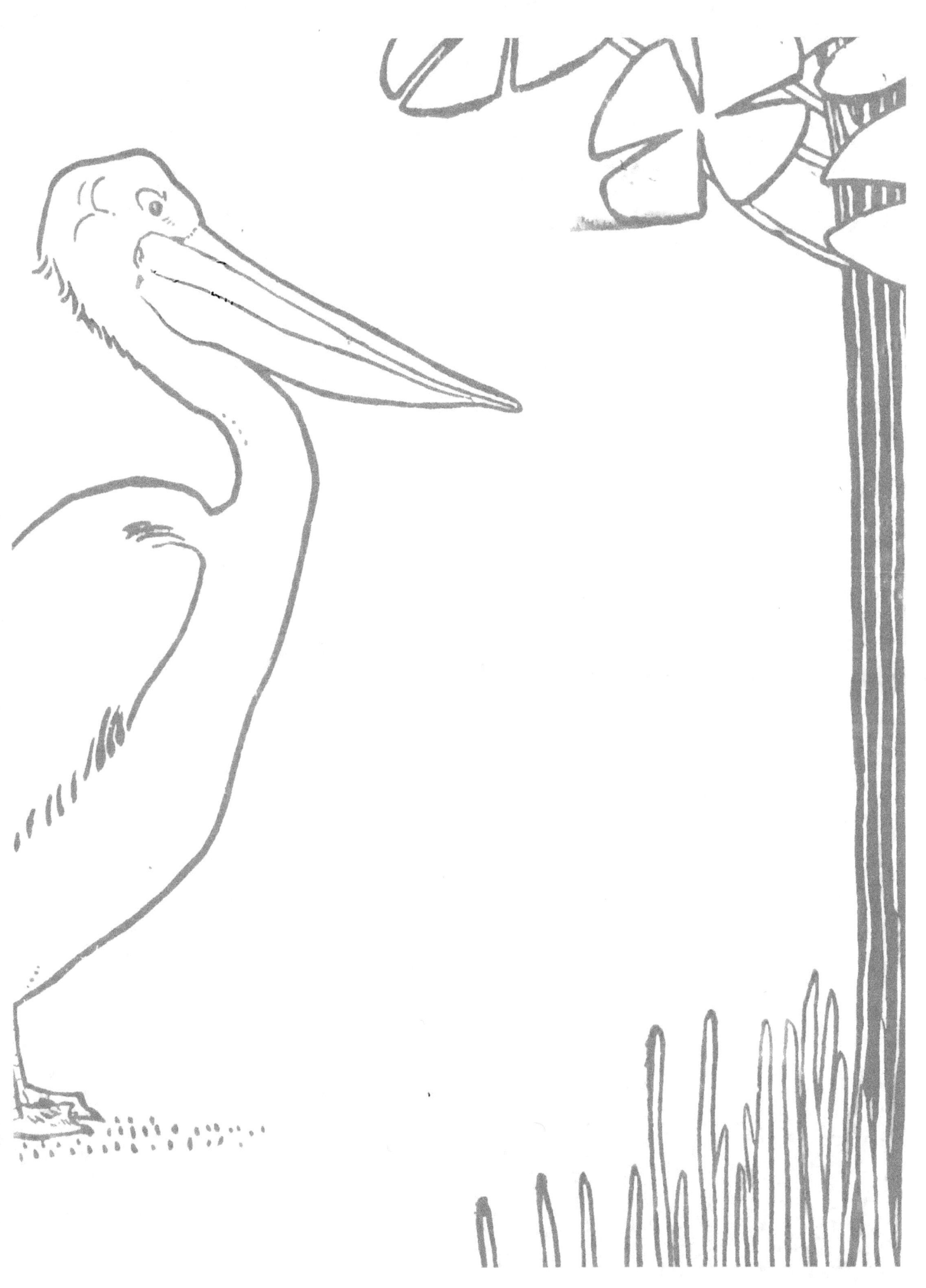

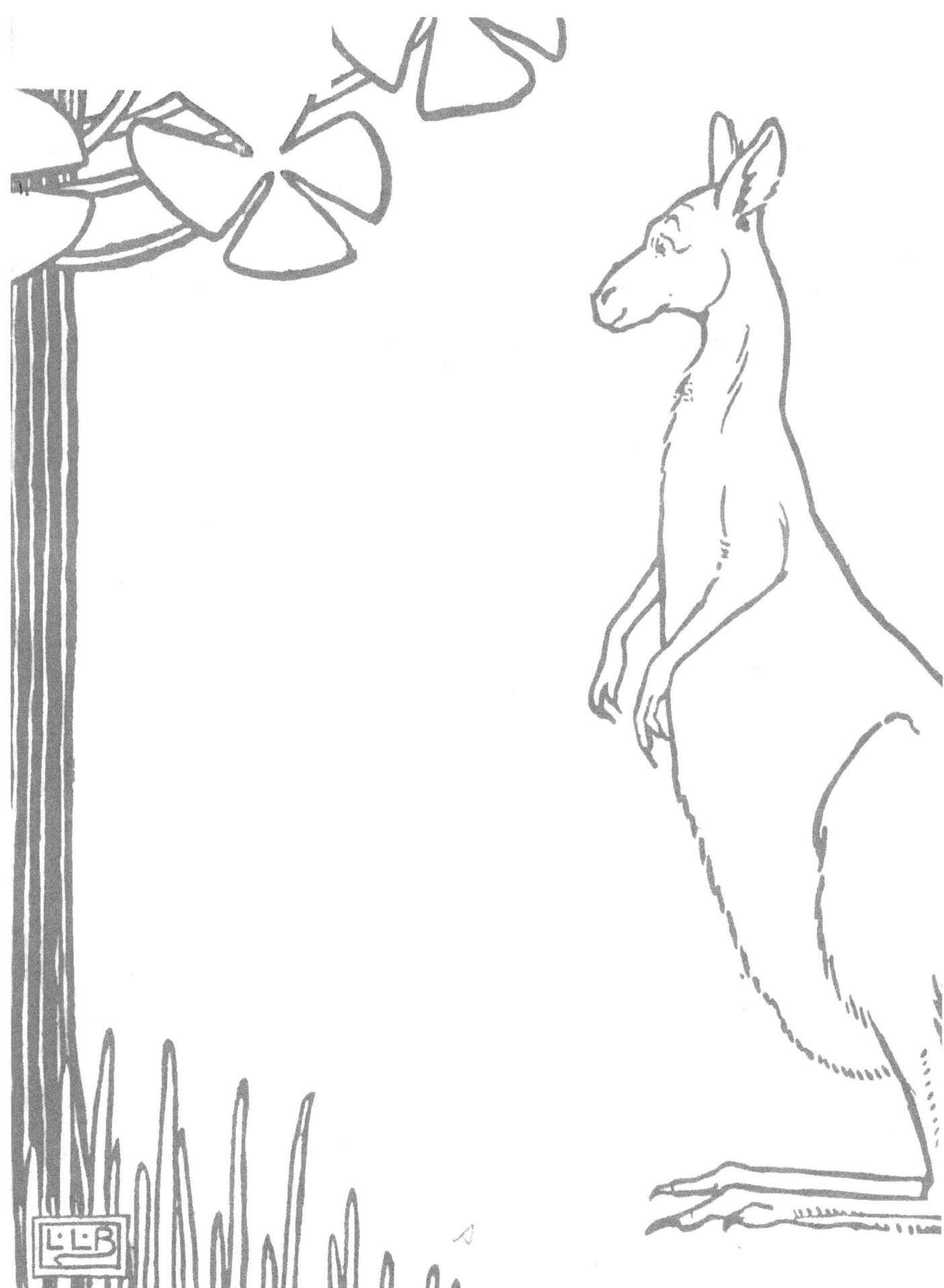

THE PELICAN CHORUS

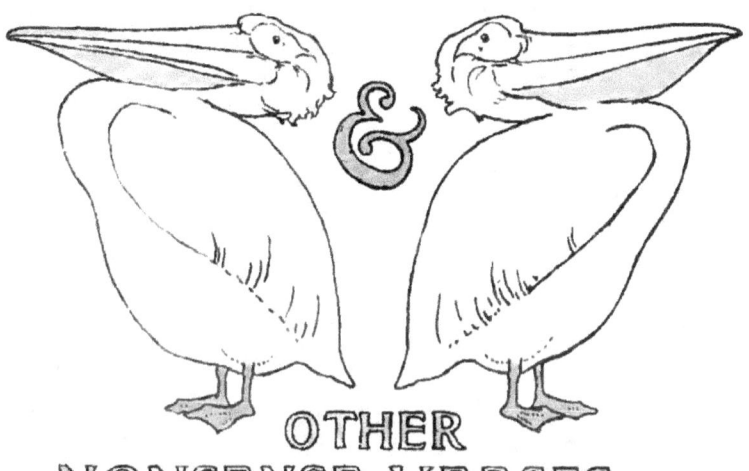

& OTHER
NONSENSE VERSES

WITH DRAWINGS BY
L·LESLIE BROOKE

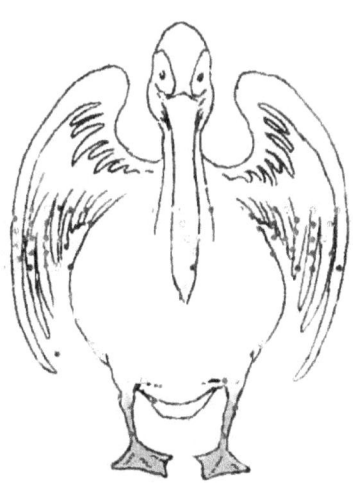

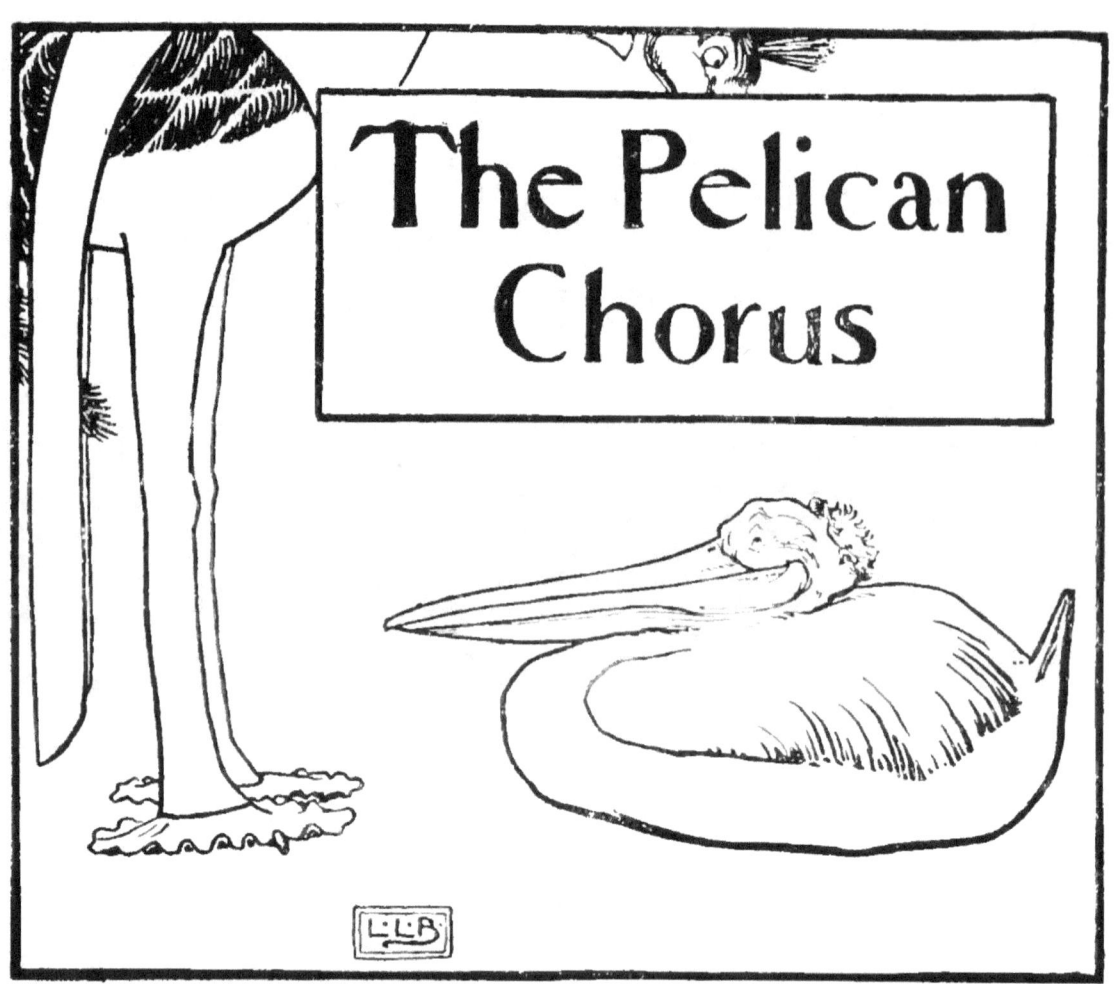

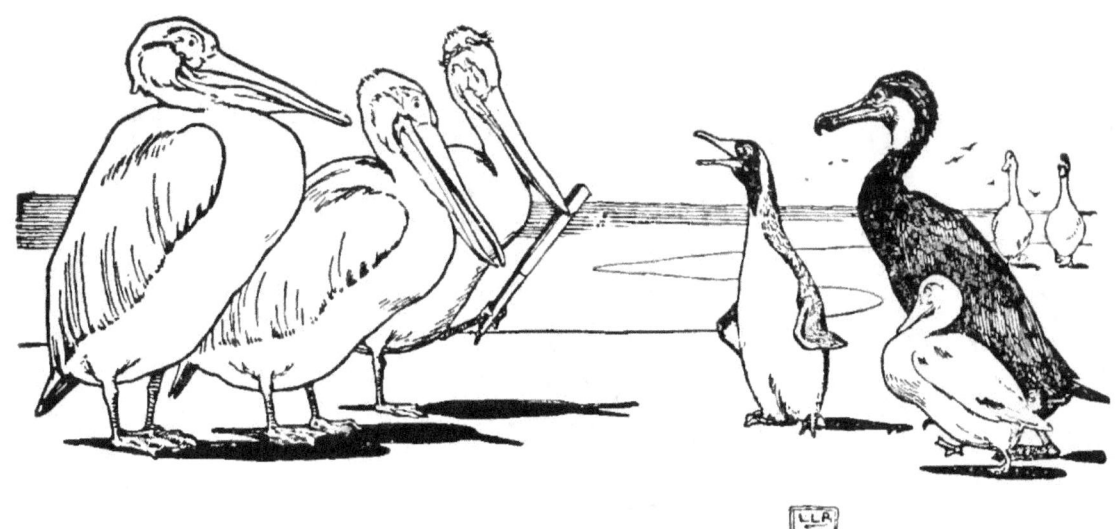

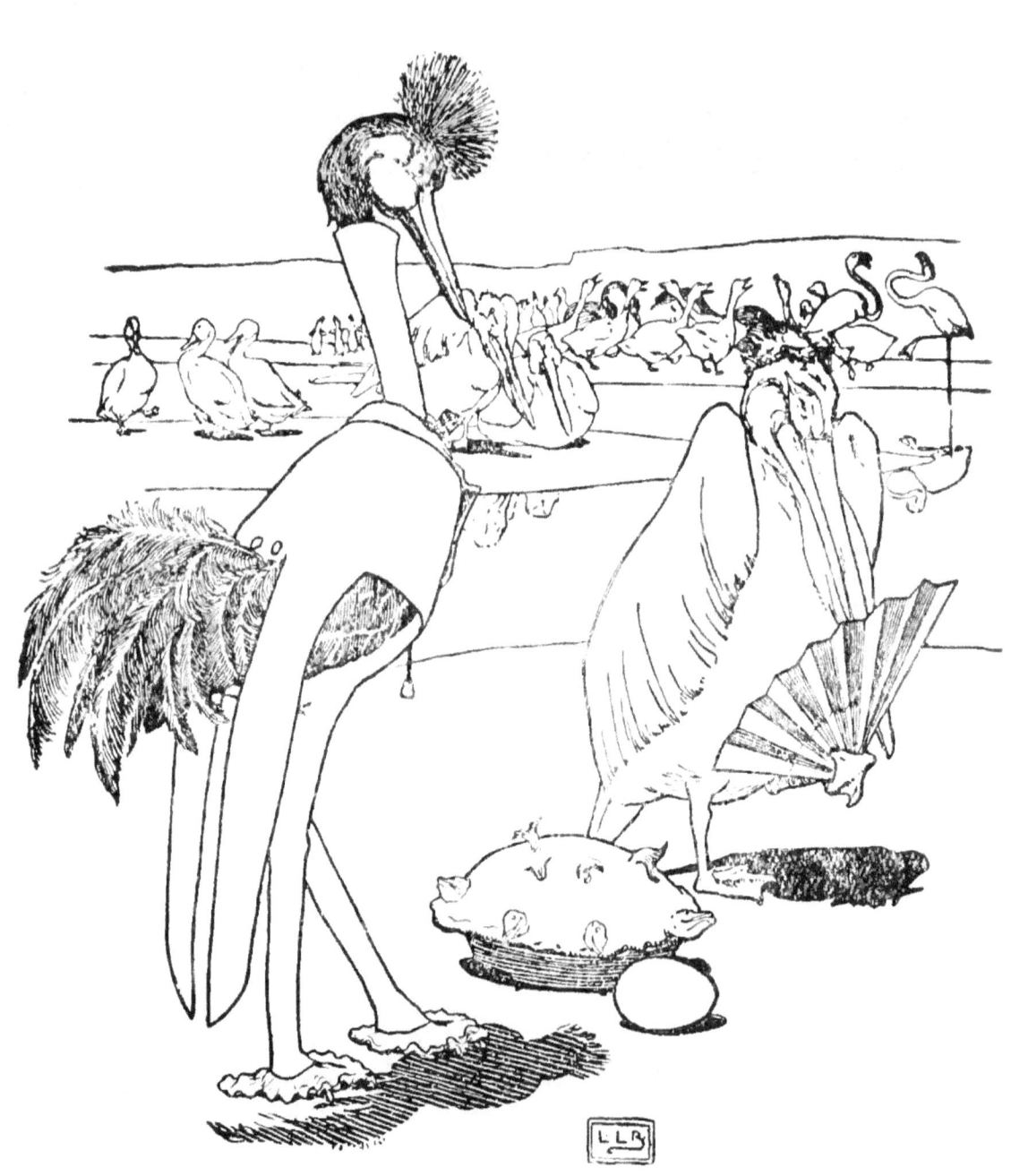

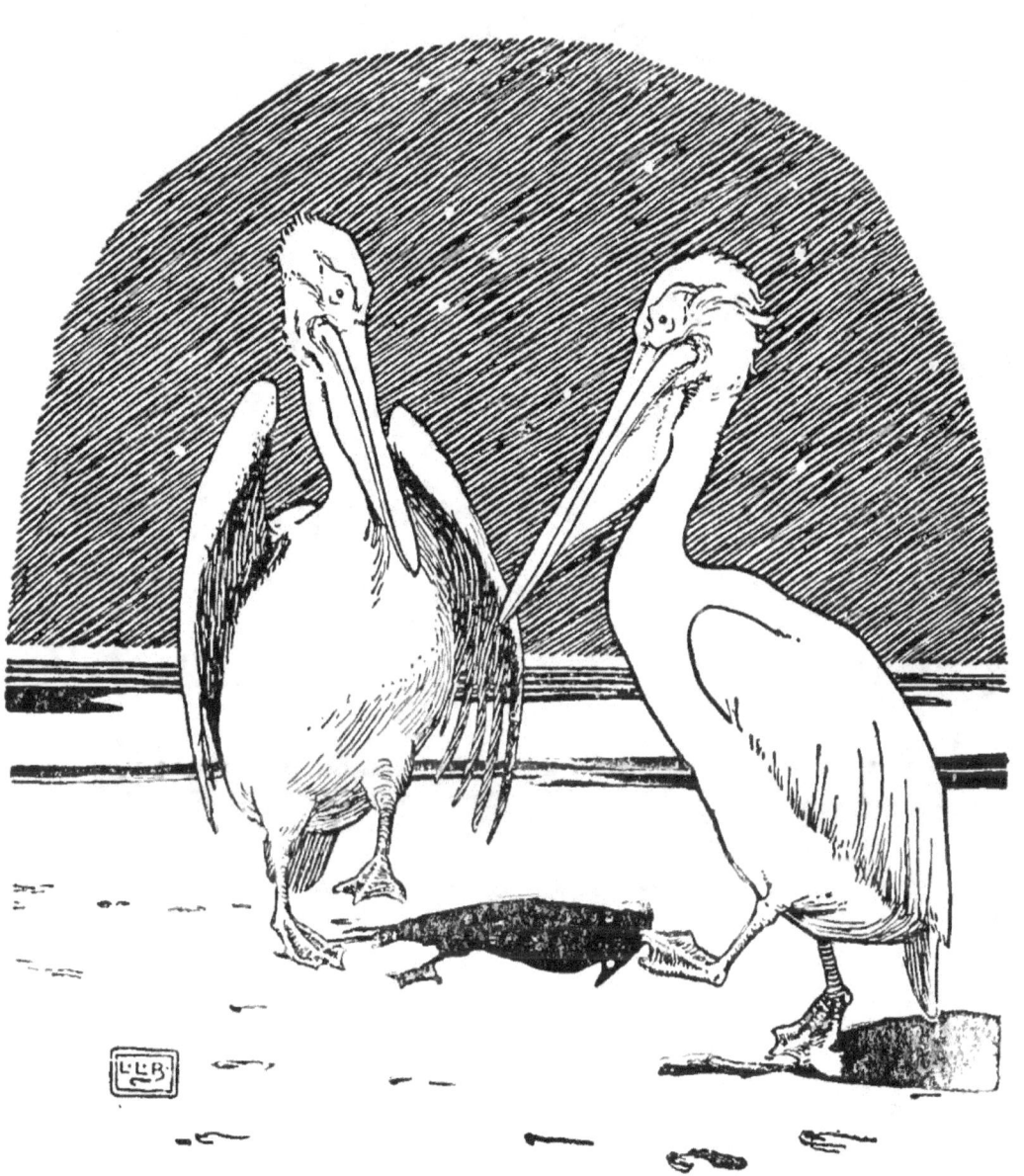

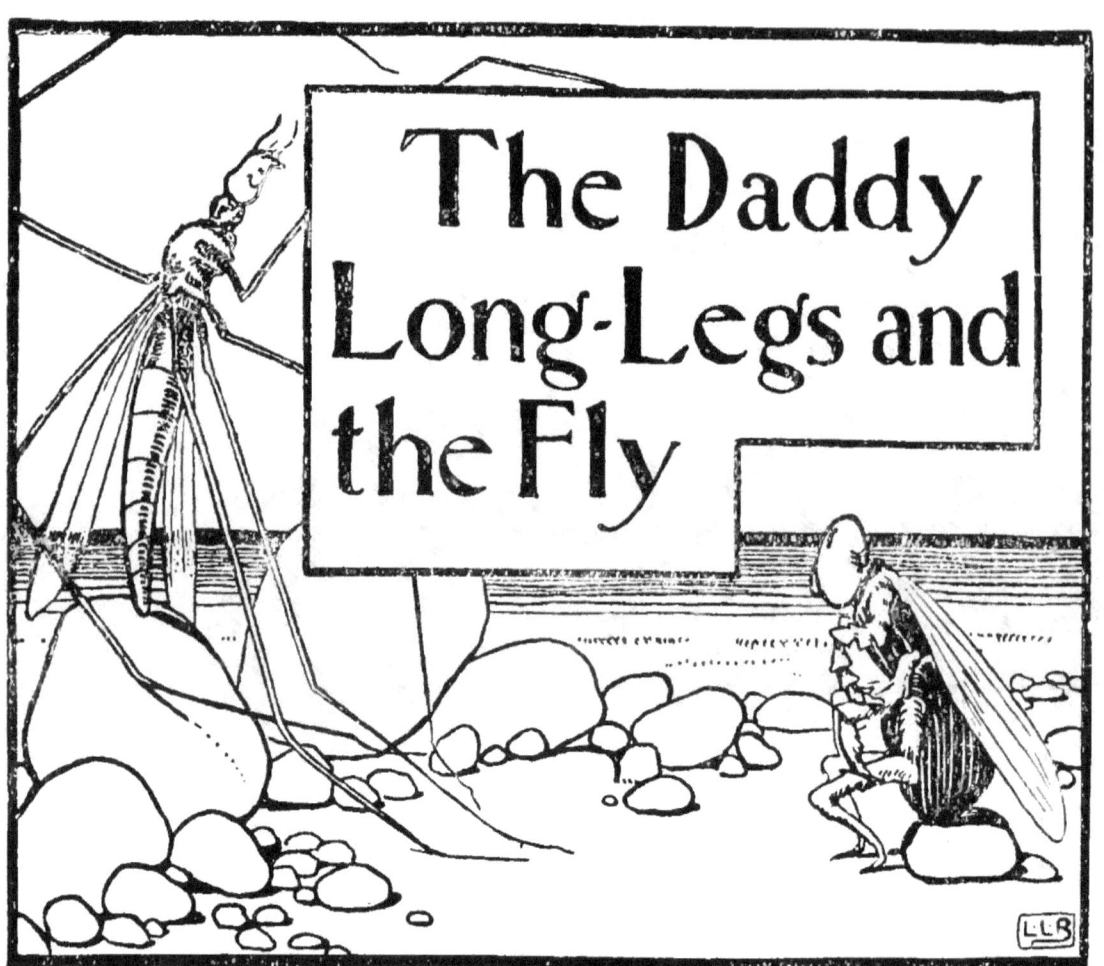

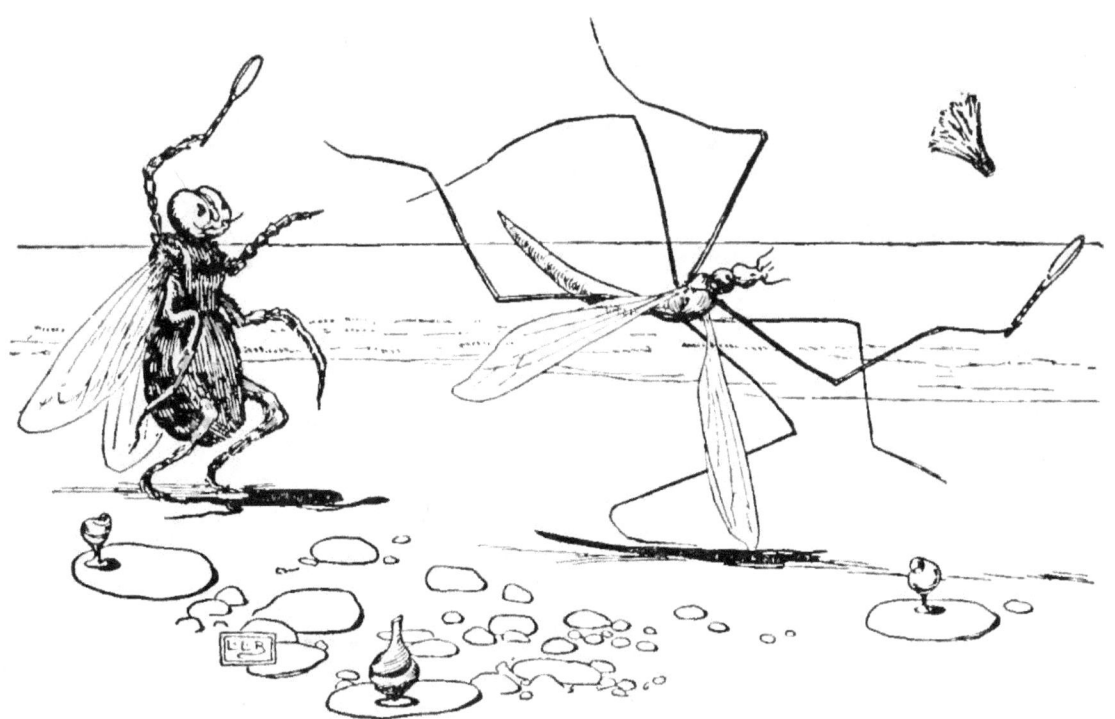

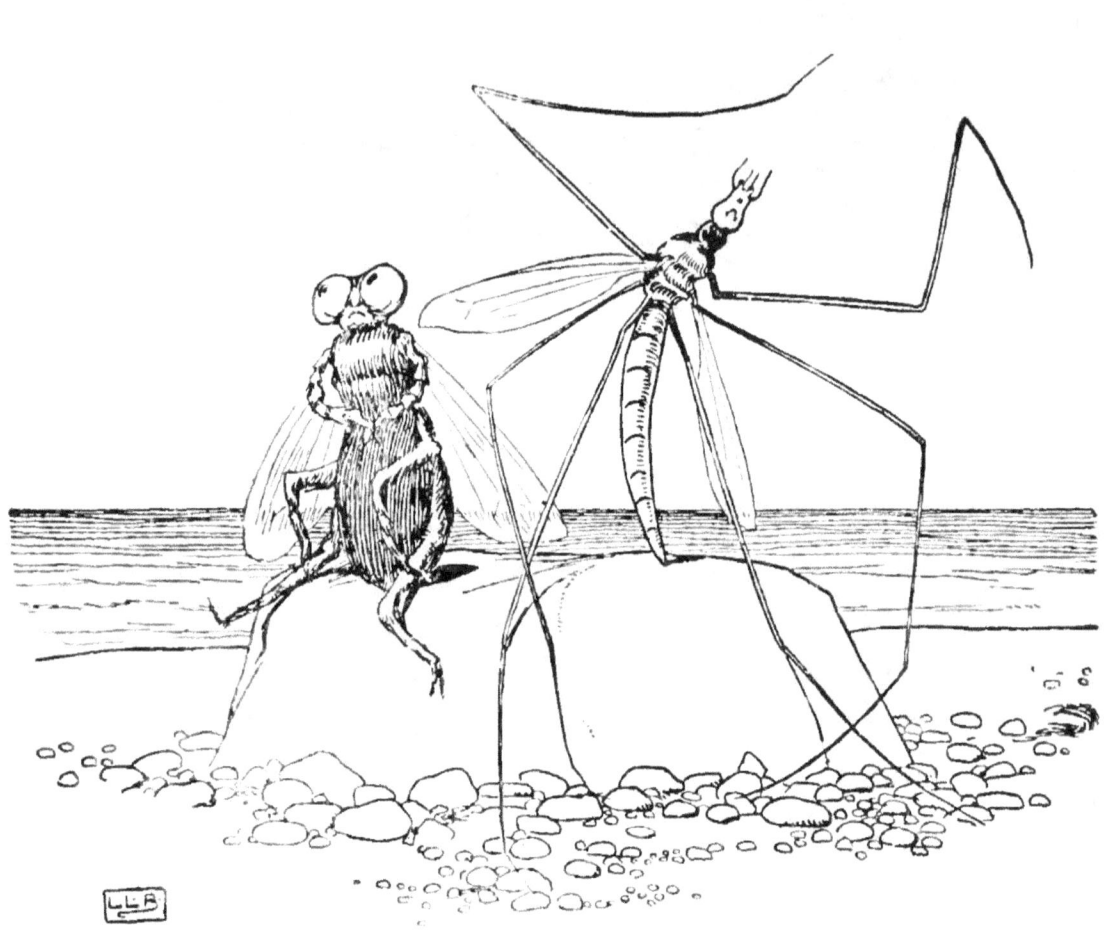

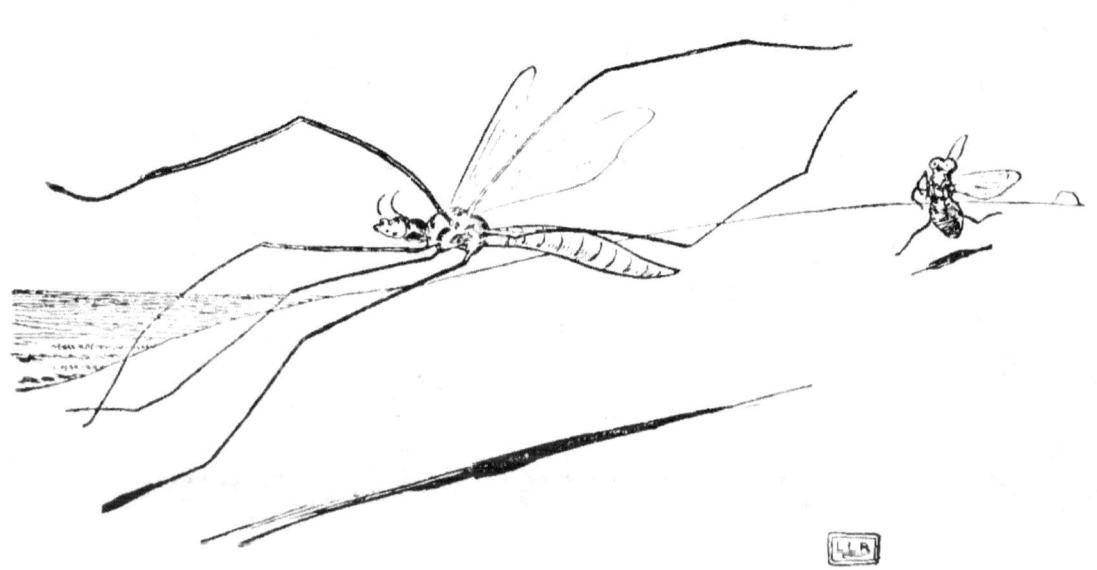

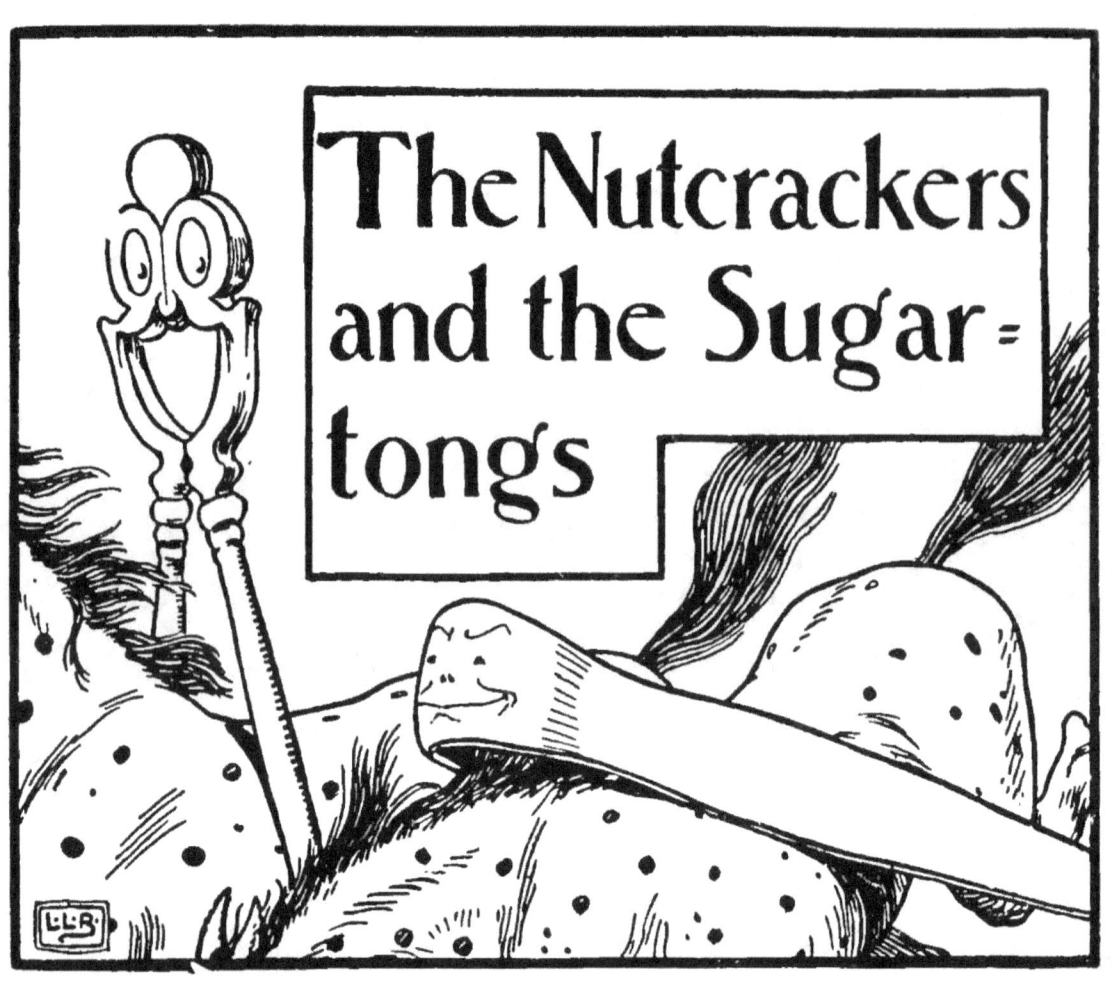

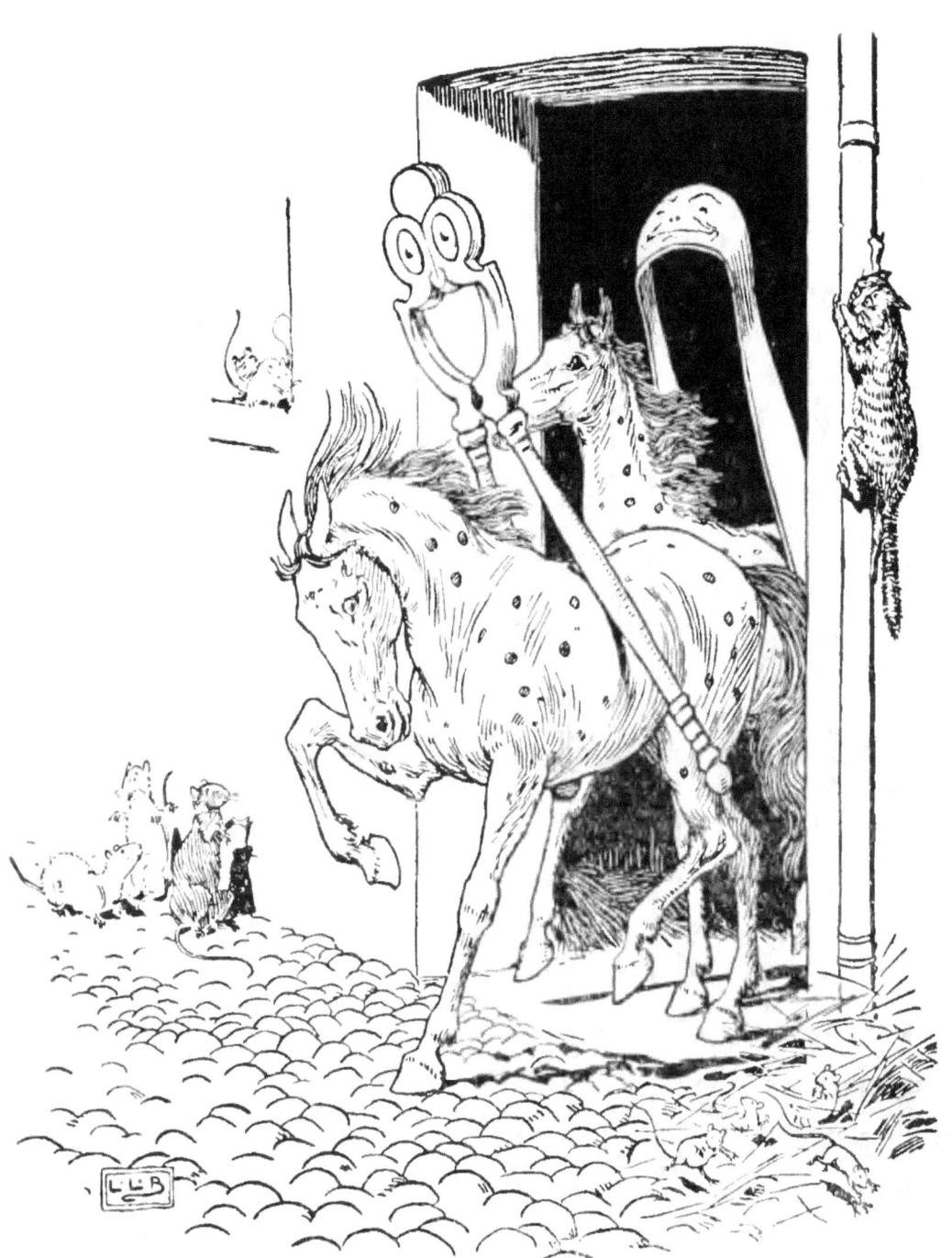

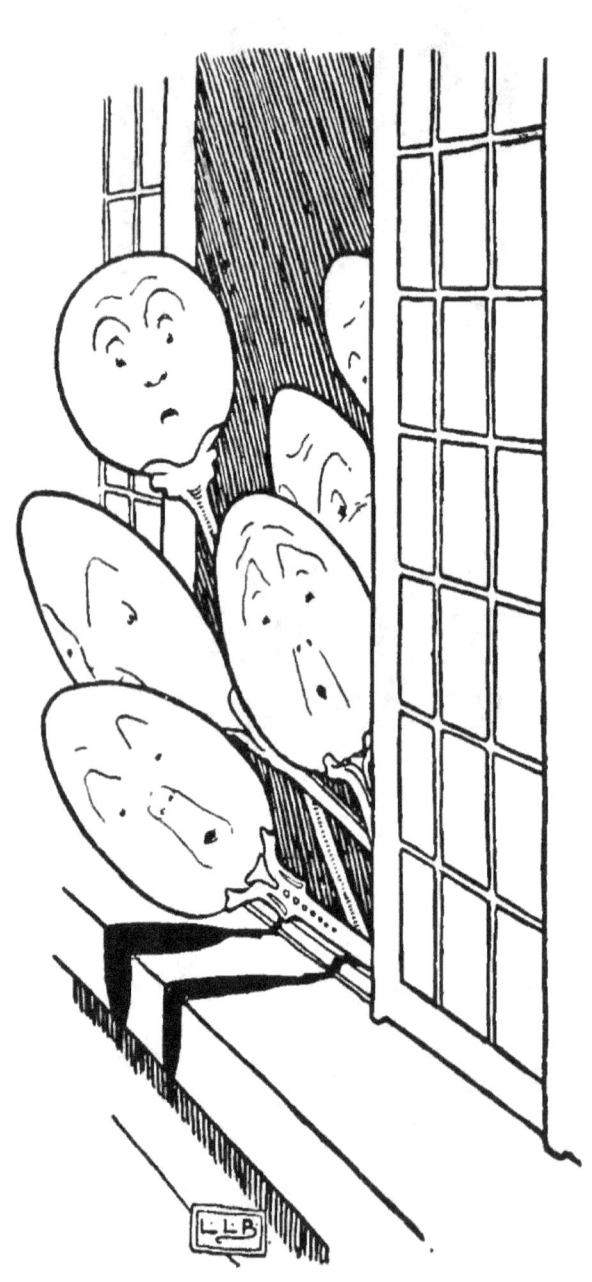

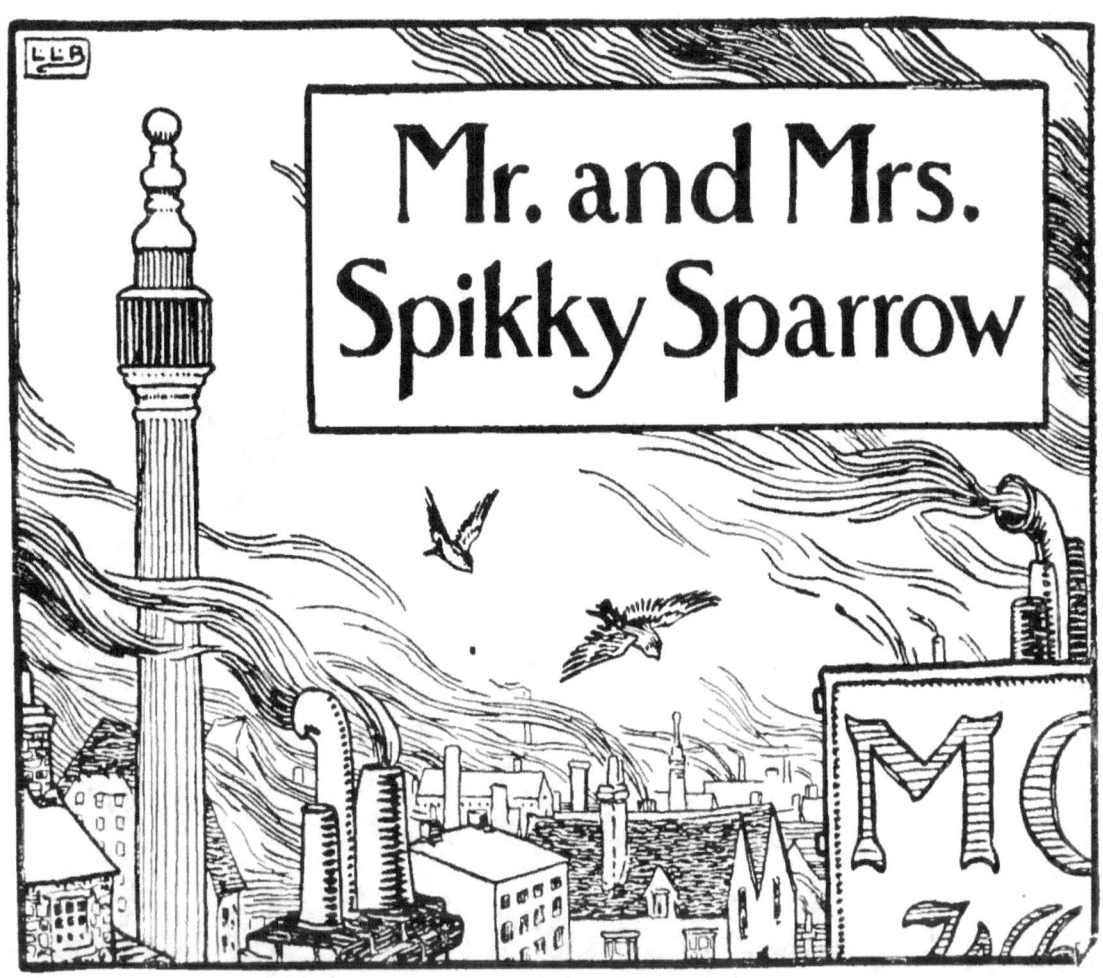

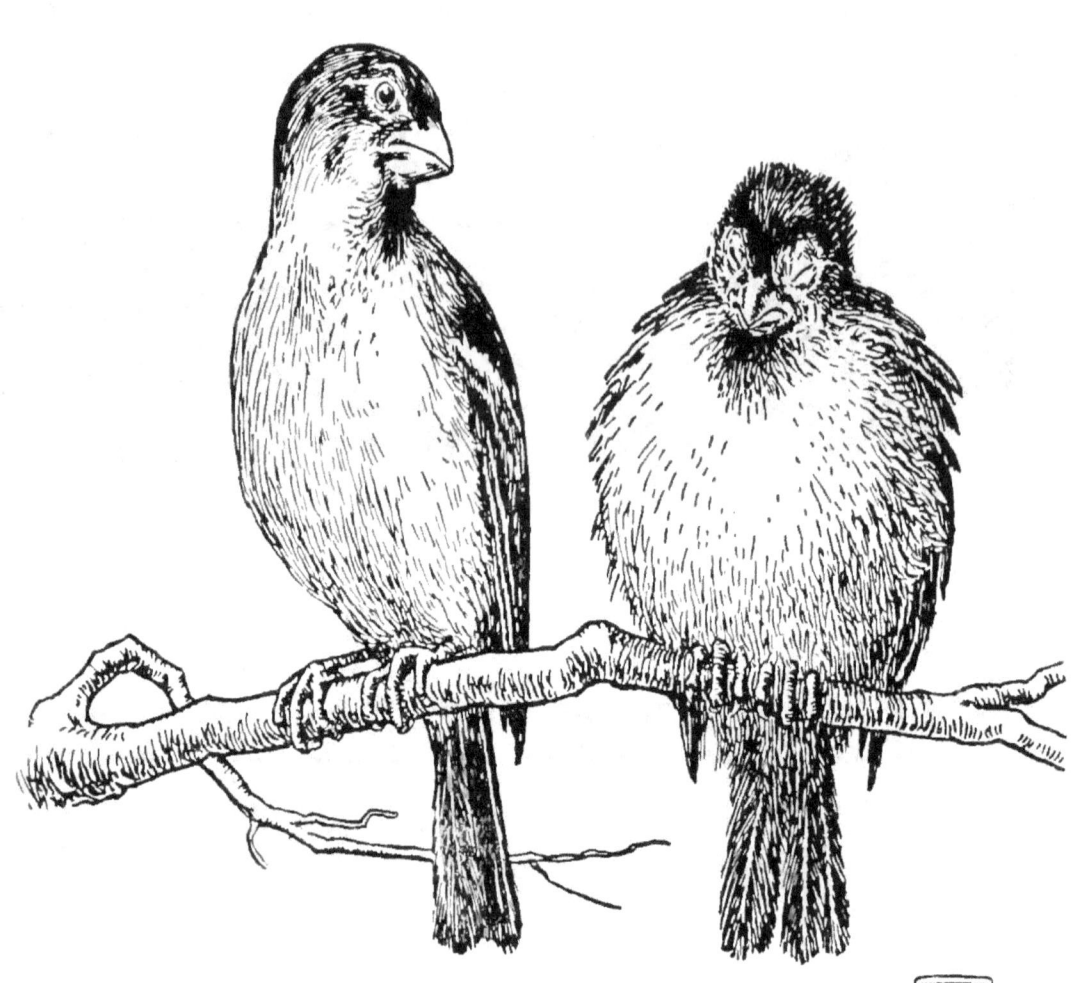

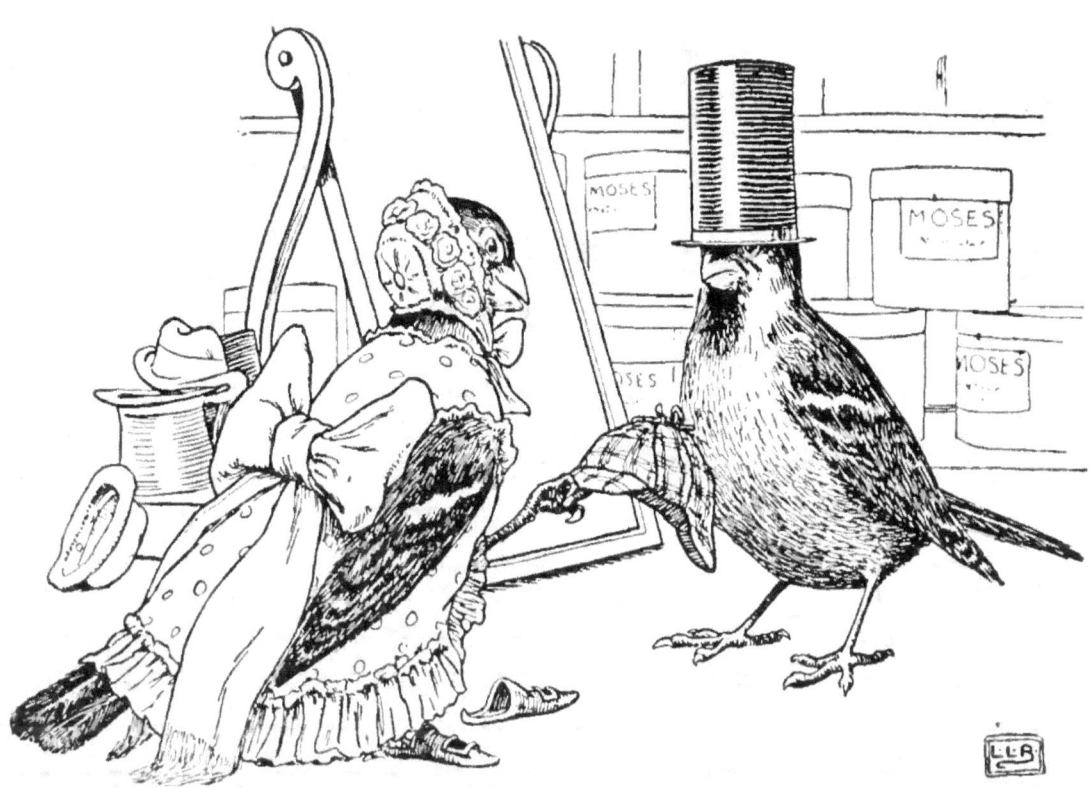

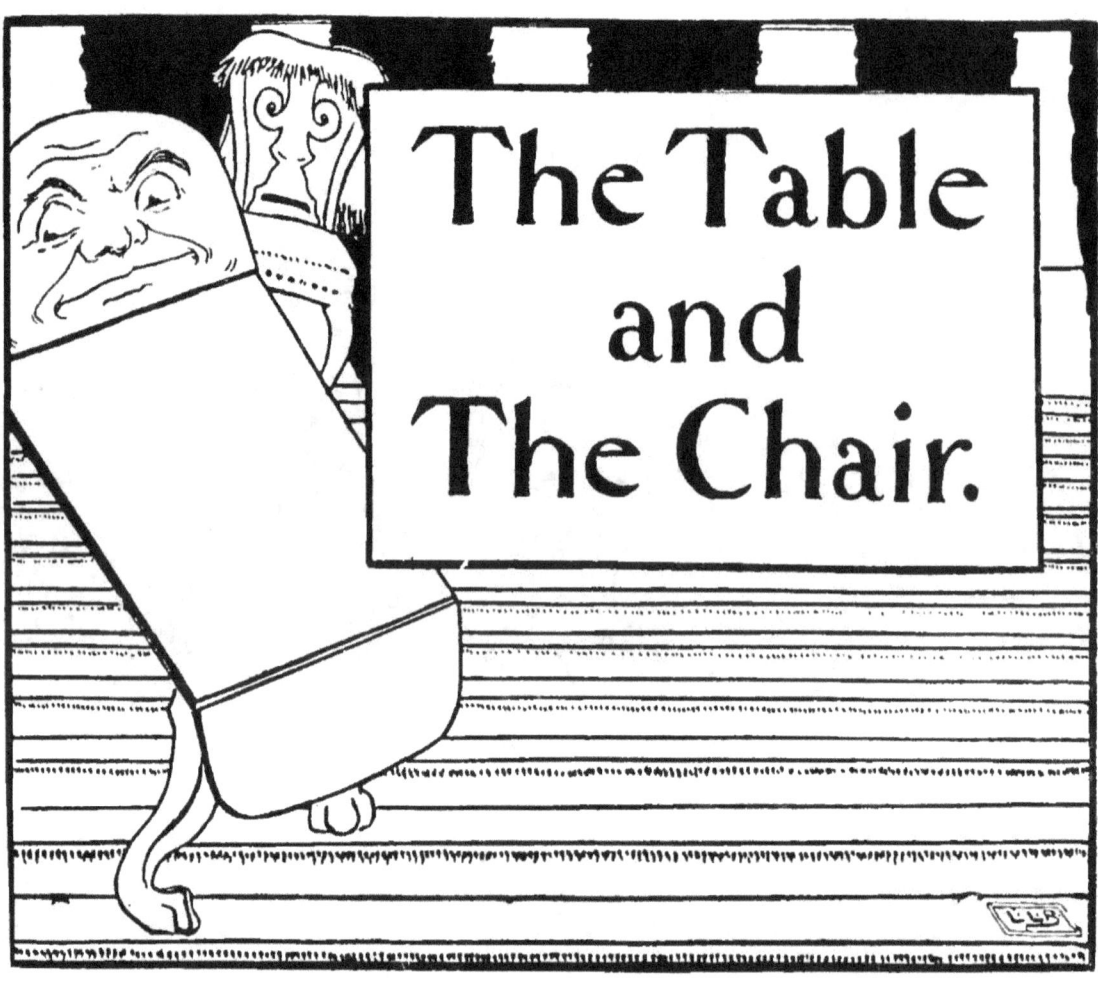

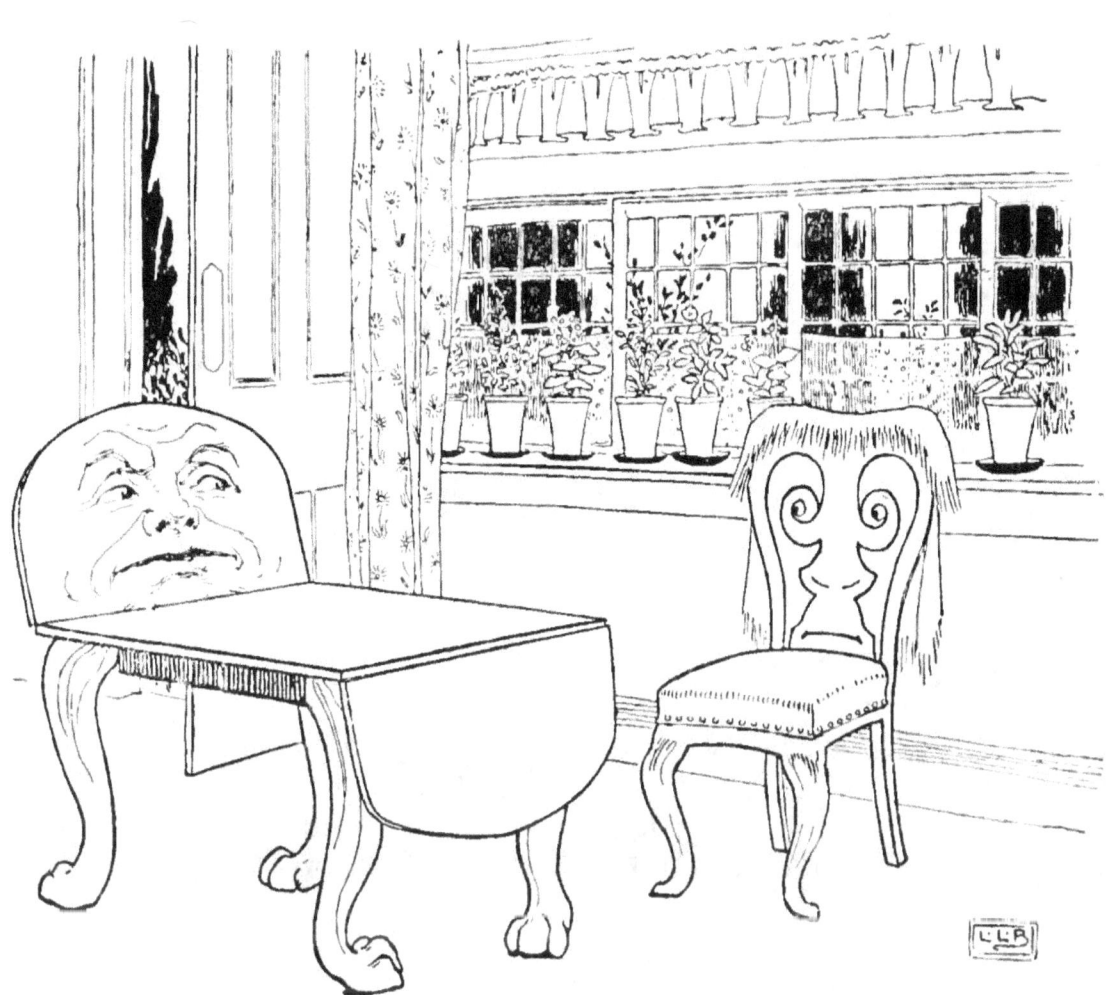

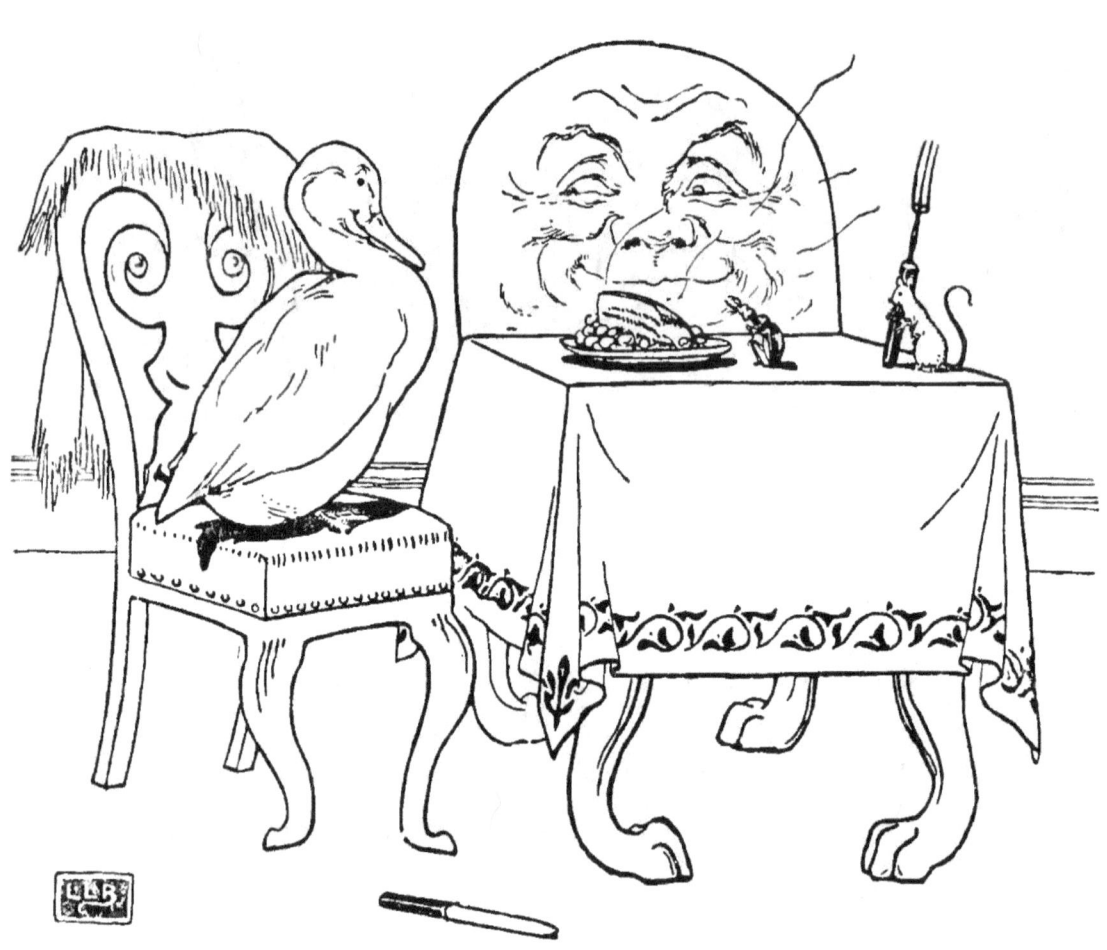

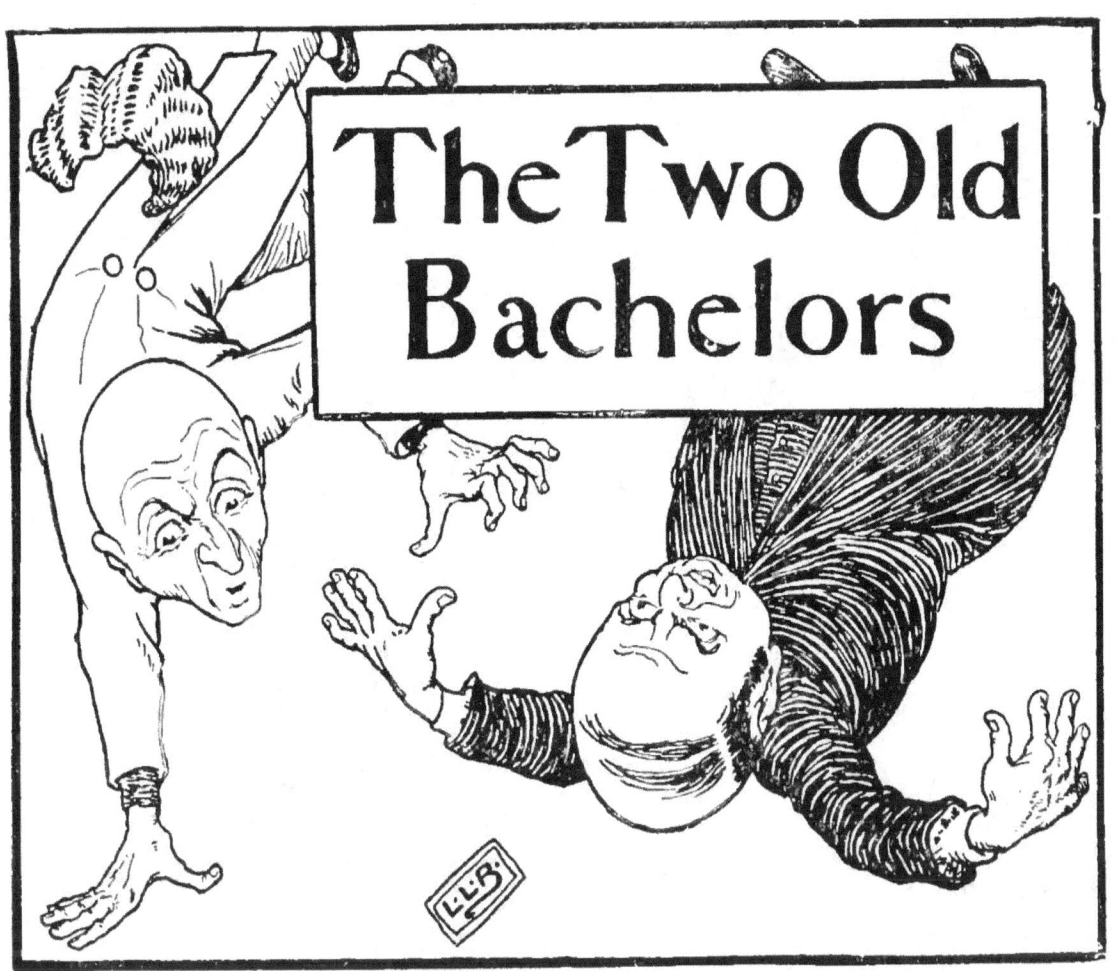

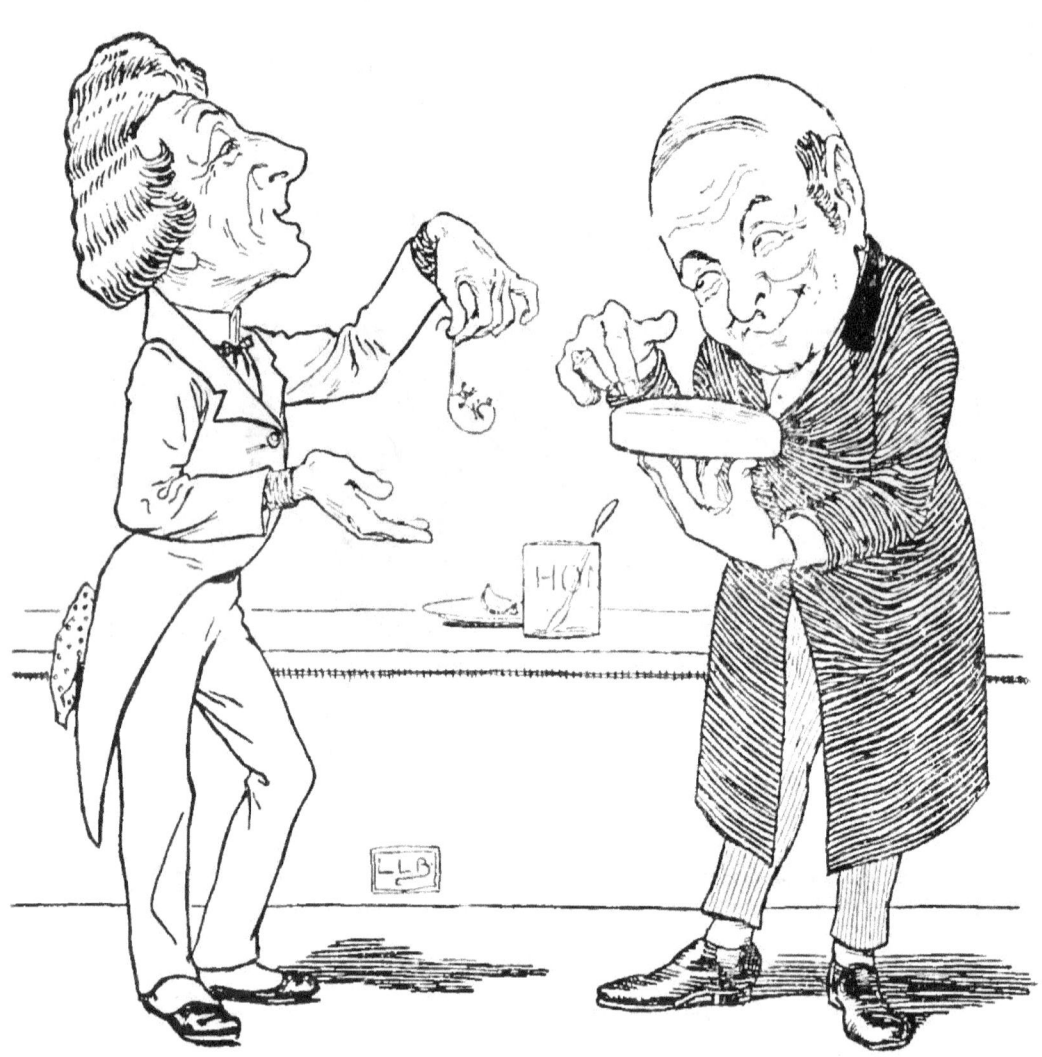

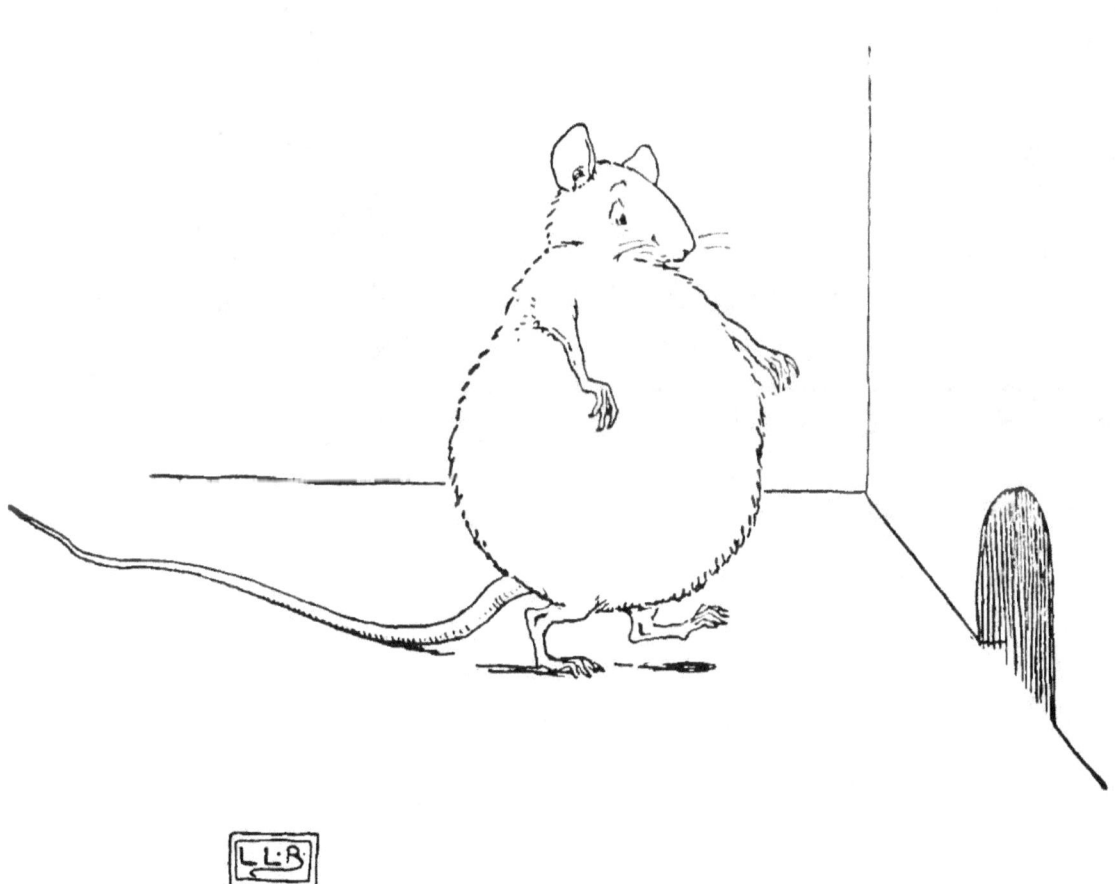

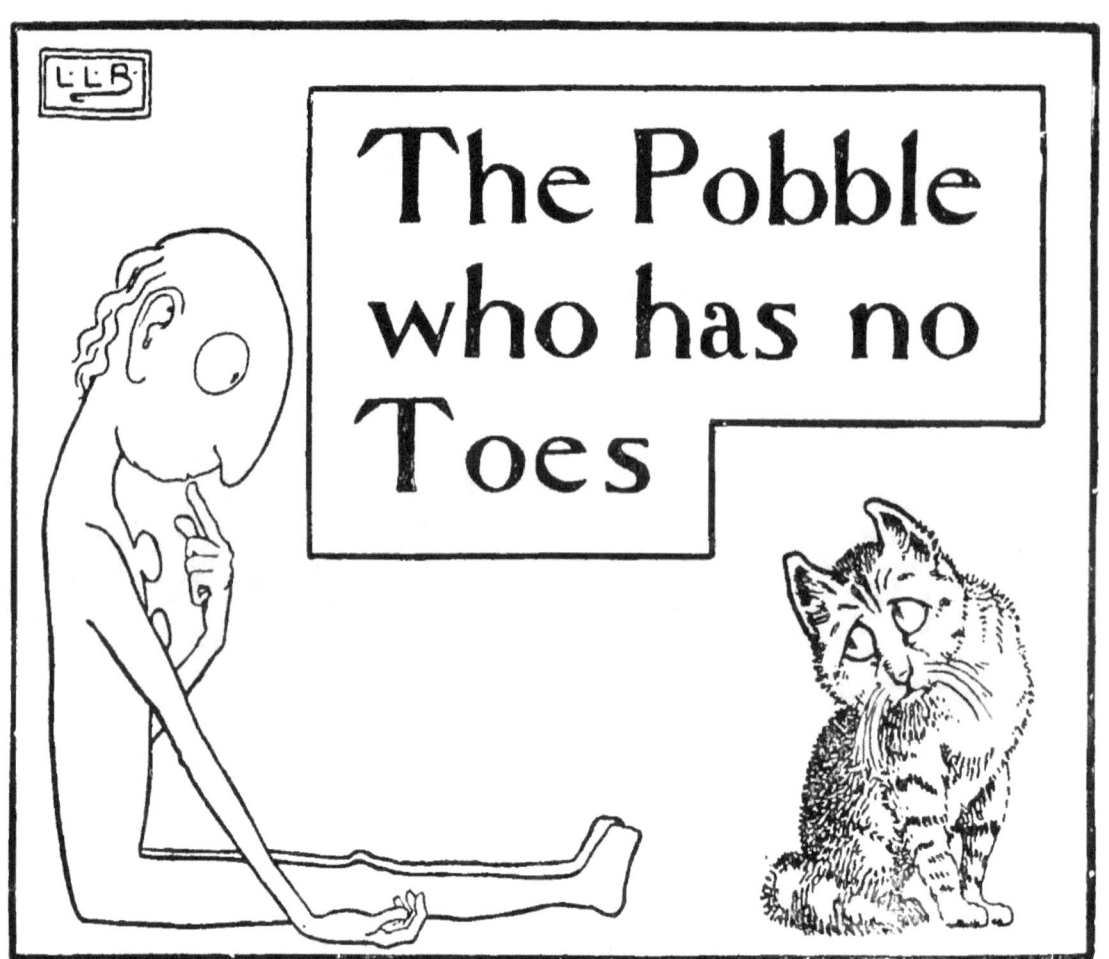

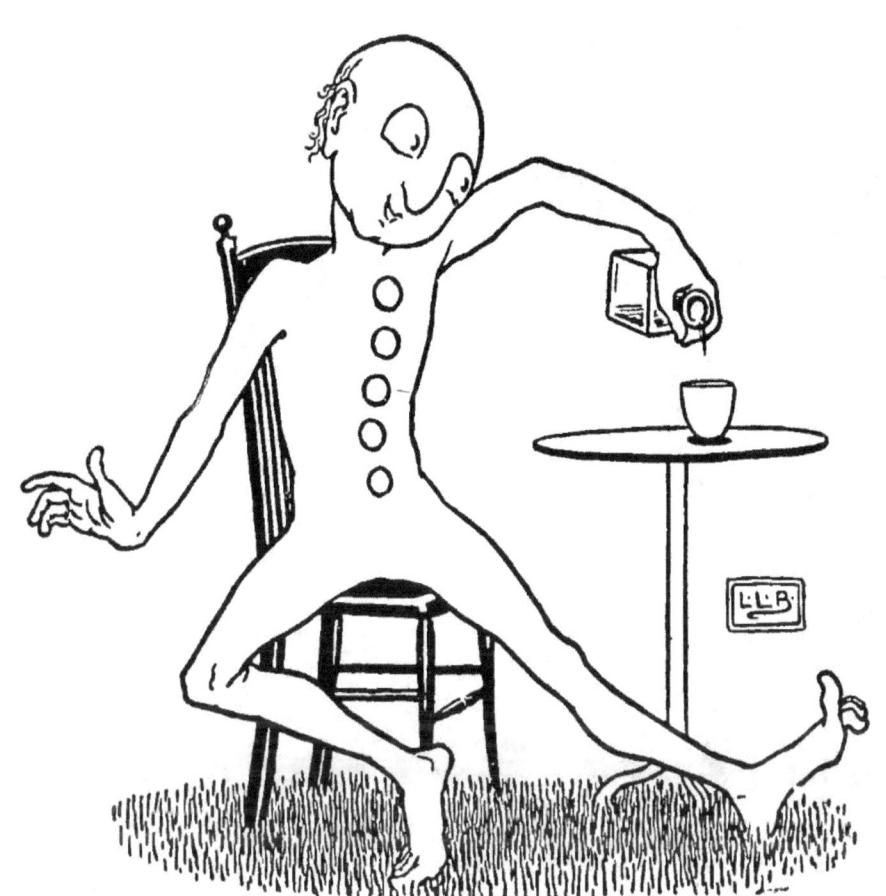

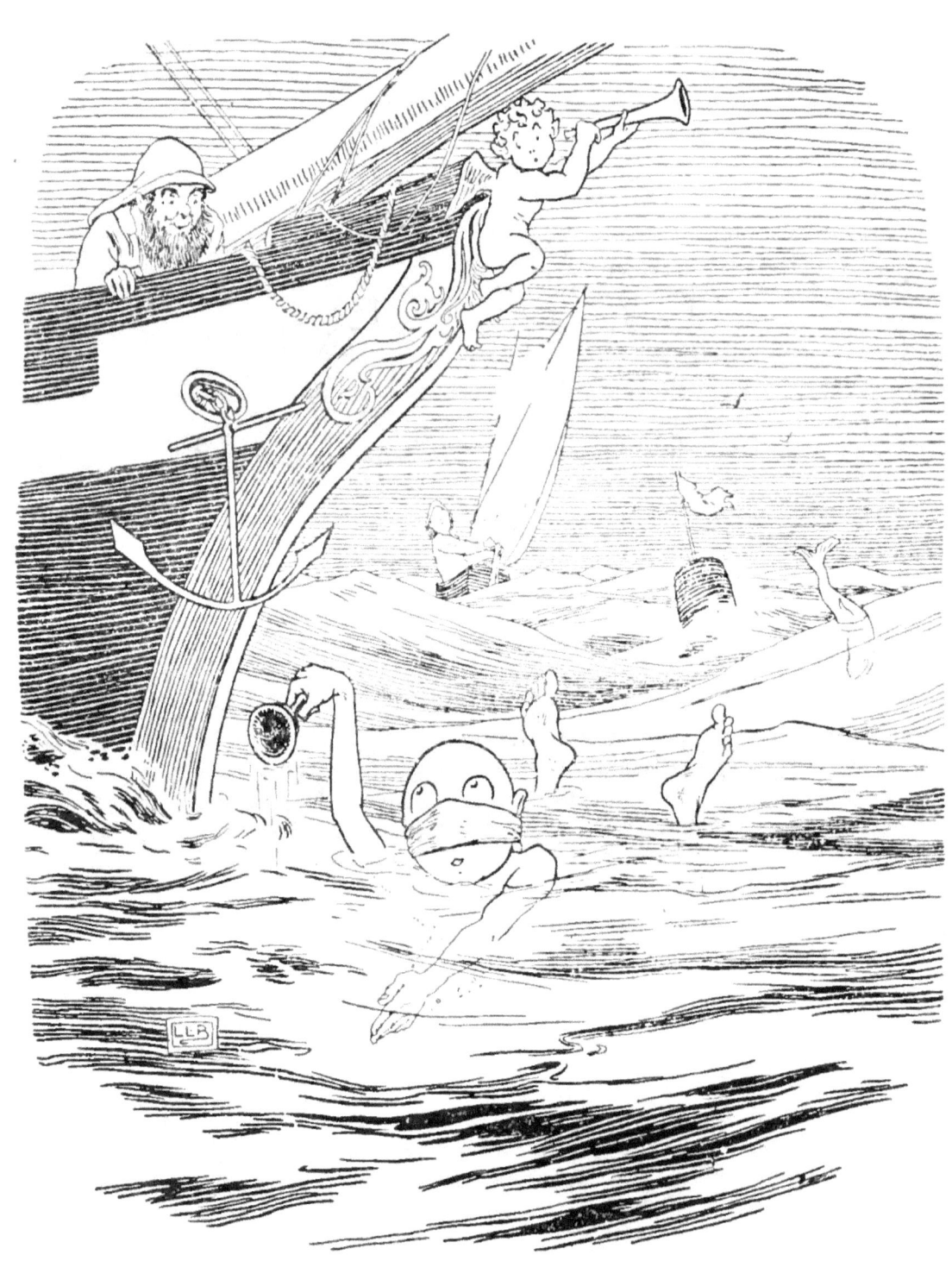

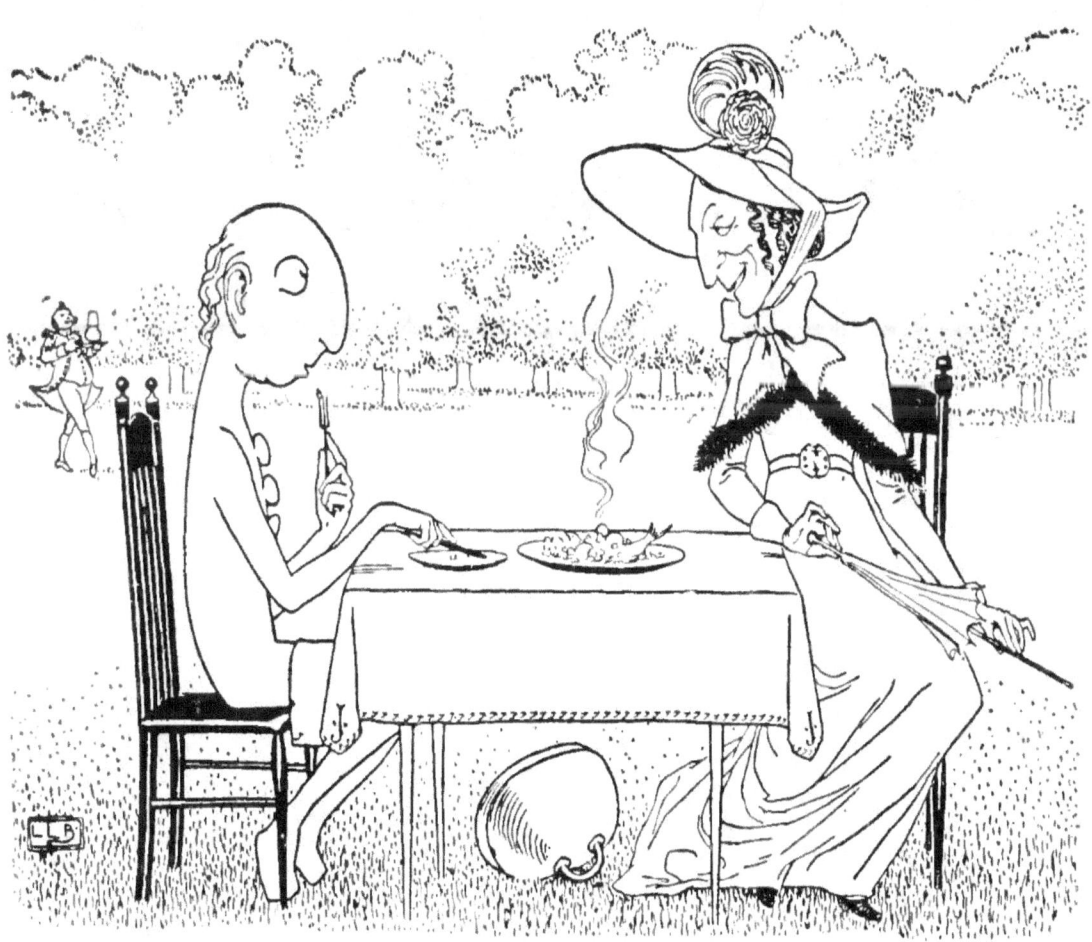

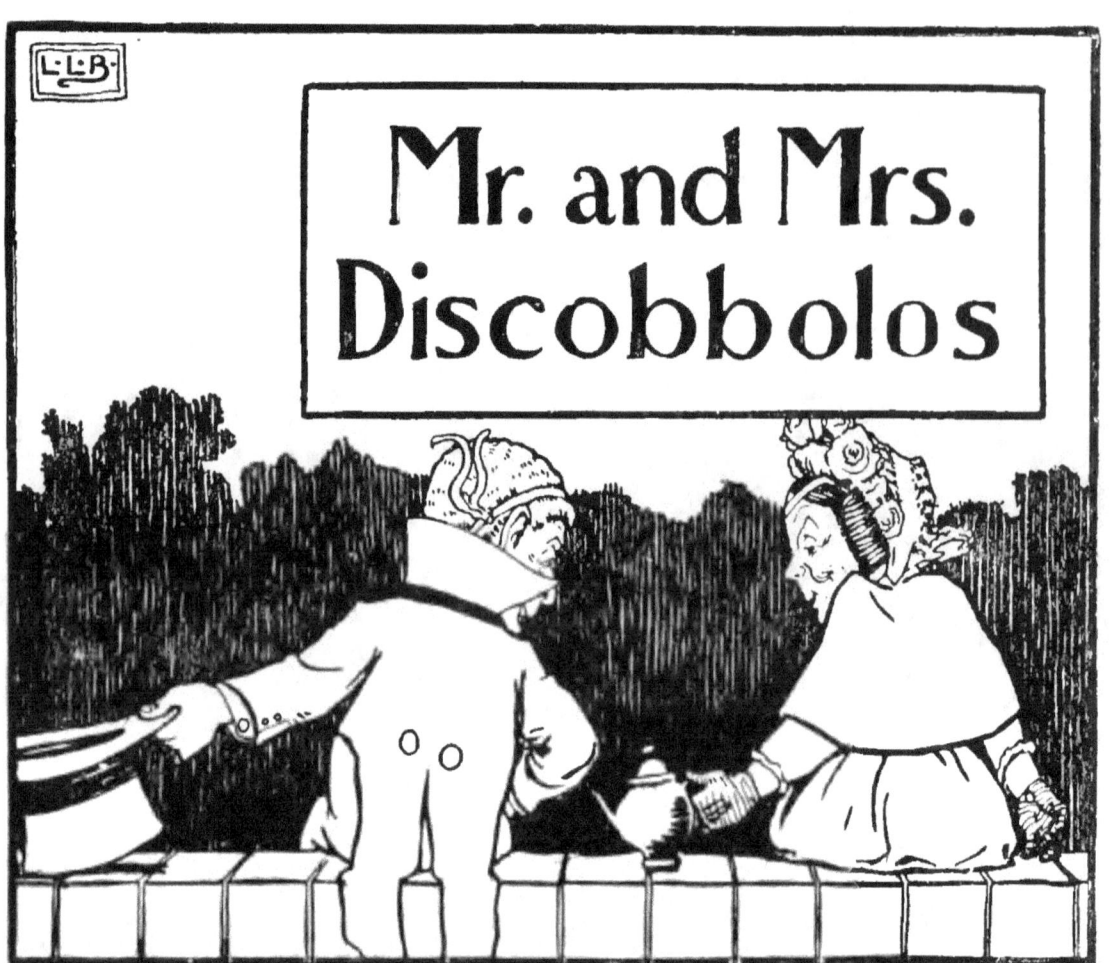

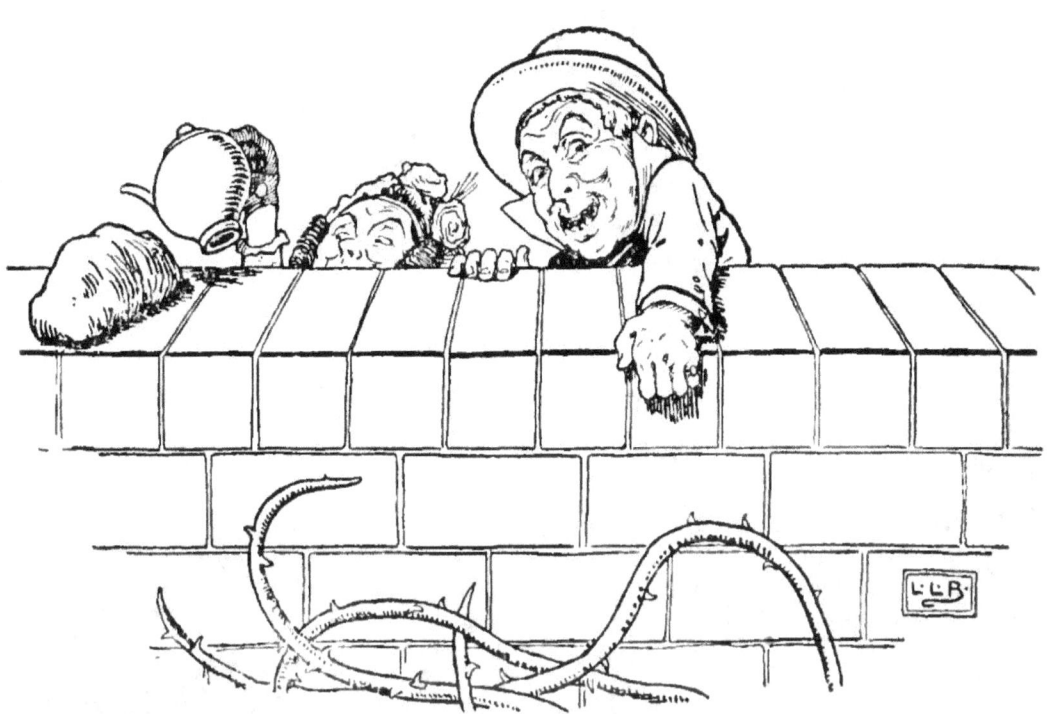

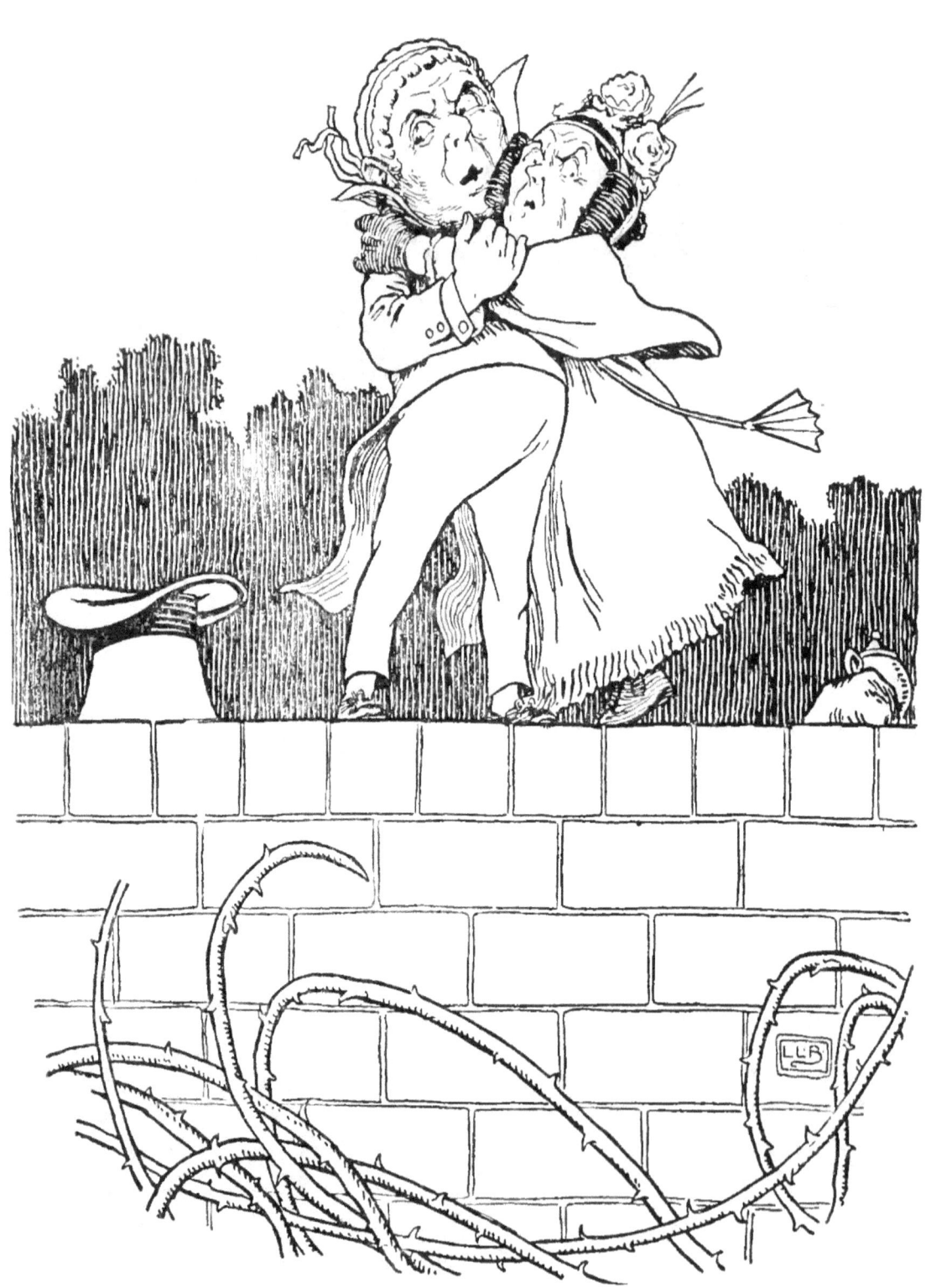

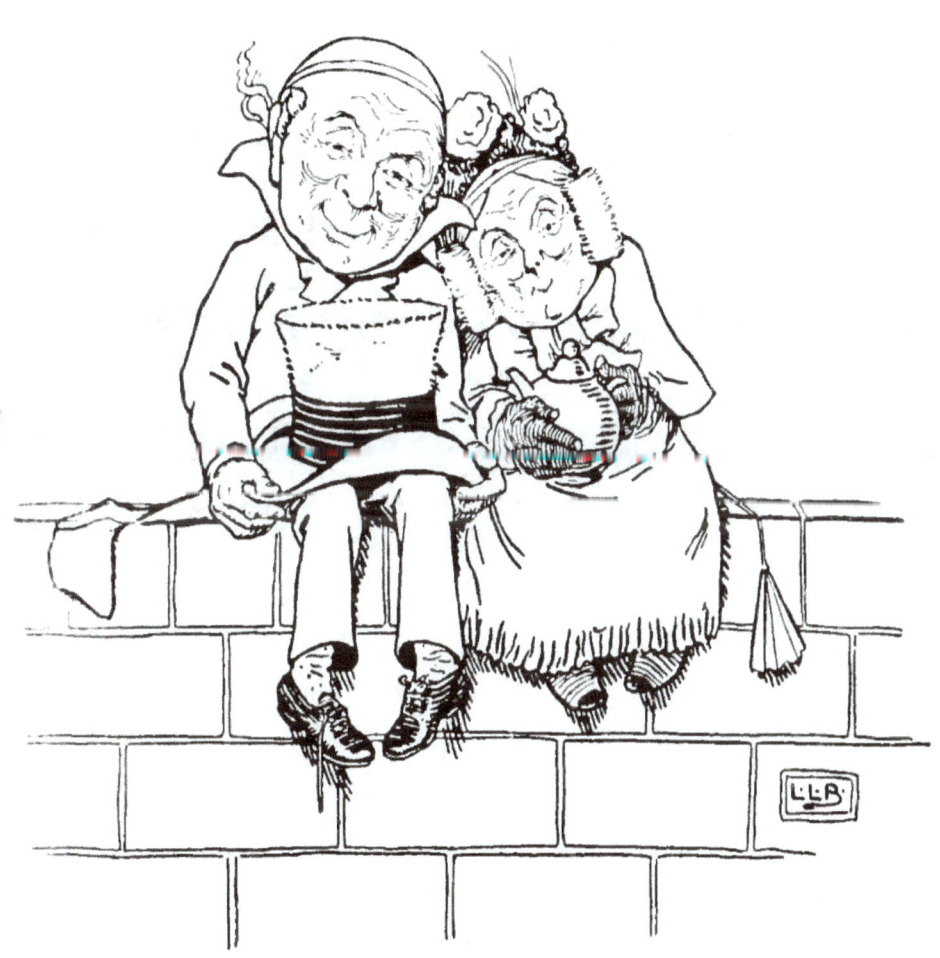

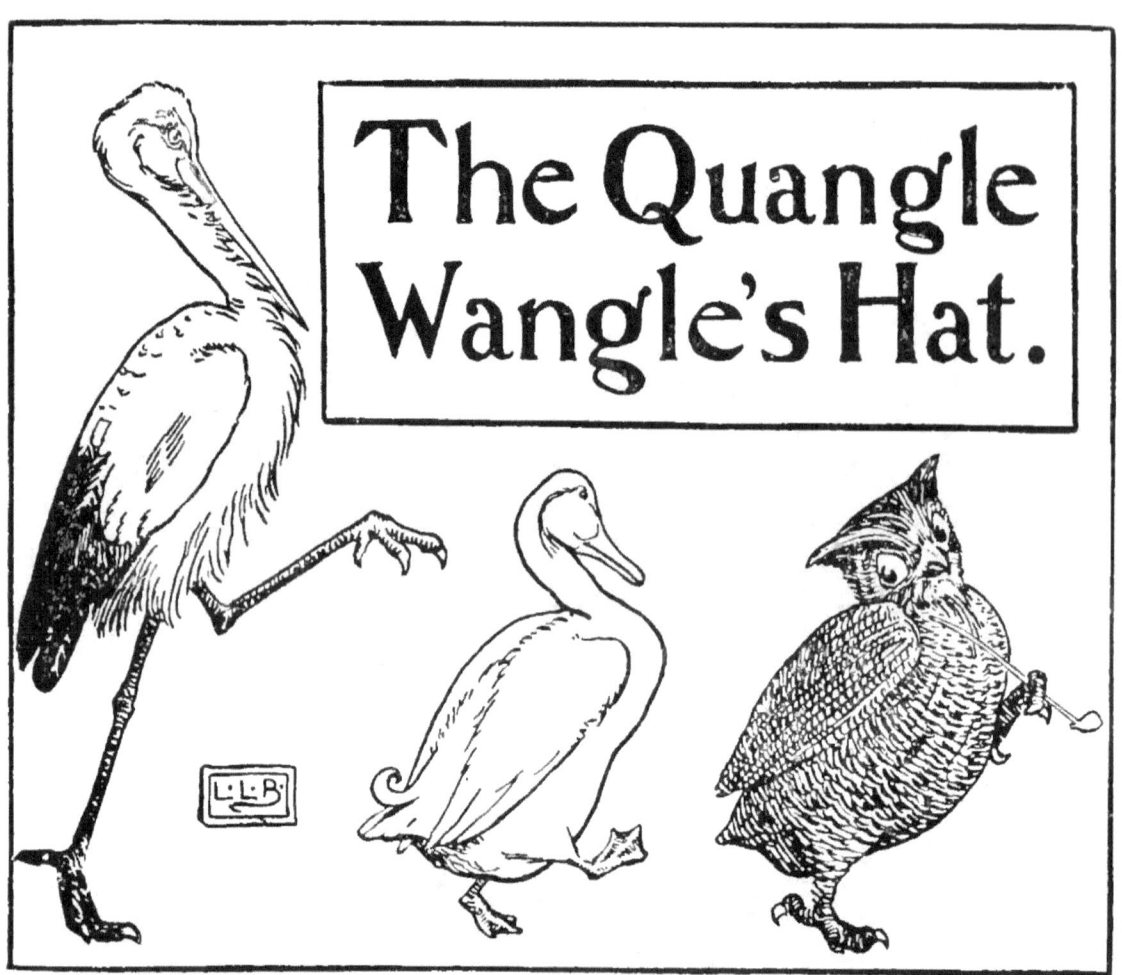

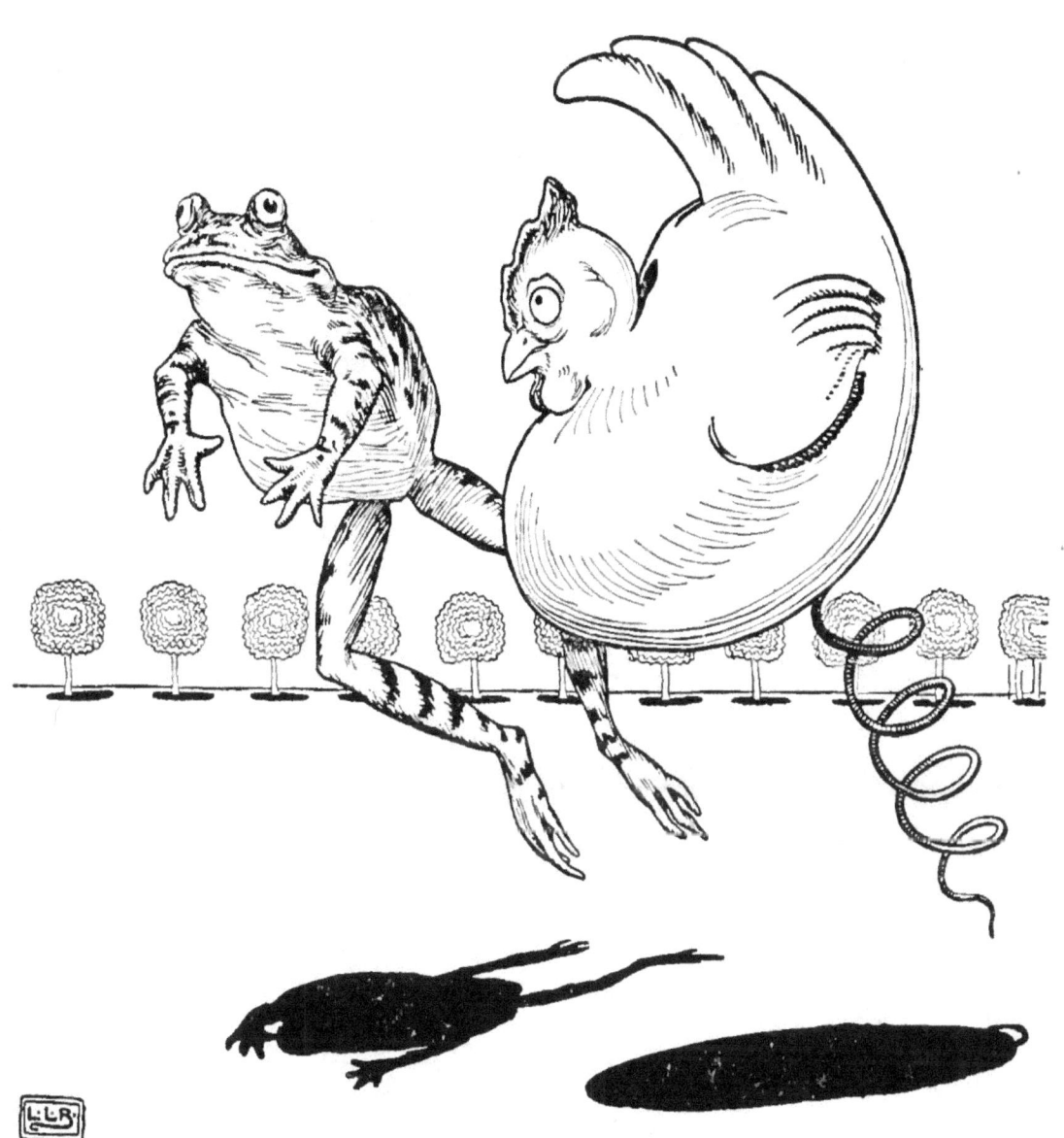

www.ingramcontent.com/pod-product-compliance
Lightning Source LLC
Chambersburg PA
CBHW082218220526
45470CB00010B/3223